Money Skills for Your Rich Life

Your Essential Financial Literacy Guide to Income, Budgeting, Smart Saving, Credit and a Debt-Free Life

Bernette Sherman

Mount Hope Media

Book Cover by Mount Hope Media, LLC

Contents

Chapter One

You Need to Be Rich

Yes, I said it. You need to be rich and I don't just mean that my life is rich with love and friends' rich. I mean, you need to have actual money.

I don't mean just enough to scrape by. You need to have enough to live like you want to live and to do the things you love to do. To enjoy life. How can you do that if you're broke? I know when I was broke, I wasn't living life to the fullest. I couldn't. I was too stressed about bills or even the smallest emergency.

How can you grow as a person and expand yourself if you can only experience life through other people? We are here to have life and have it more abundantly, and we can't do that if we don't have enough money to more than meet our basic needs. Not in this world.

I say this because money impacts every other area of your life. I don't care what anyone says about money. When people don't have it, they feel that lack. They feel it not just in their wallet or bank account but by the things they are missing out on in their lives. It's why people feel like money alone will solve all their problems. Who doesn't want more money to make all of life's problems vanish?

And that feeling is right. Not in a money is everything way. Not in a greedy way. But in a 'money is the currency to get what we need in a world that uses money', kind of way. People aren't trading chickens, goats, or furs for food and a night on some hay in modern society.

Money is an answer to many of the problems people face. It can solve issues of having enough food, clothing, a place to live, or a car to get to work and other important places. It can boost self-esteem because, in our hearts, all of us want to contribute to the world in some positive way. You can be charitable when your financial needs are met and you still have more.

Ask a random person on the street if they would like to have an extra ten thousand dollars in their bank account that isn't just to pay bills, or if they would like to keep their bank account the same. Any sane and honest person would want the ten thousand dollars. Why? Because they know it can buy security, food, shelter, and joyful experiences. It can give them richer experiences.

Money is a way for us to know our contributions are valued. Money lets you go to the doctor when you're sick, take care of personal hygiene, and buy the sneakers you need to stay active. It lets you show your love to your family or friends with a nice meal out, or having the funds to get groceries to cook at home using appliances and utilities that money pays for.

Having enough money lets you be comfortable, decreases stress and illness, and can improve your relationships. More than enough money lets you enjoy yourself, reclaim your time, have new experiences, and allows your money to grow.

In the world we live in, money is a necessity. It allows you to have a rich life. Please don't misunderstand me. I don't mean having a rich life only in the sense of dollars, but also in the quality of your life. Everything I mentioned in the examples above is part of the quality of your life.

Money determines which car you can buy and whether you're clicking your heels three times and crossing your fingers every time you go to turn it on, or know it's reliable with features that let you be comfortable on your commute.

How much money you make or have access to determines which neighborhoods you can afford to rent or buy in, as well as the quality of shopping and overall investment that has been made in the neighborhood. Businesses consider household incomes as well as the number of homes and residents before deciding to put in a business or invest.

This is why the book you're reading now is so important. You need money for a rich life, but just as much as you need money, you need money skills for your rich life.

What many people don't realize when they start earning money or their income increases, is that money is only as good as you are with it. We can't be expected to know how to manage money if we've never done it or had it modeled to us by parents, family, or friends. If you didn't grow up accustomed to having money, you'll have to learn to be comfortable with the responsibility of managing your money.

And if you were like many of us who didn't take a personal finance class while in school or as a young adult, you may not have the skills. All of this is to say, go easy on yourself. You are here now, and because you need to be rich, you need to build money skills for your rich life.

Chapter Two

Vision of Riches

Most people are given only what they can handle. When they're given more, they often wind up back where they started. They can become millionaires for a year, and then it's gone because they didn't change who they are or their mindset around money.

When money is tight, it's easy to be tempted by promises of easy money. Before jumping into get-rich-quick schemes, it's important to build yourself up to be financially responsible and to have a consciousness that can hold onto money you earn so you can build a secure life and even a rich life.

Did you know that nearly one in every three lottery winners will eventually declare bankruptcy? It's a staggering statistic. It happens to be more than the average American who didn't hit the lottery.

We hear all the time, not to let money change you. Well, it shouldn't change who you are at the core, but it will change things about you. Remember, the quality of life you want? That's a change in your life made possible with money.

The key is to let money flow into your life due to the intentional changes you make within yourself over time, along with better financial and life choices you make as a good steward of money. When you do it this way, the change doesn't seem so much like a change, but more like a natural progression. You mature and earn it.

Before diving into the finance fundamentals, I want to discuss being patient with your progress and intentional about acting on what's in this book. Why? I'm confident that if you act on what I share here, it will change your life.

Patience and Growth

Wealth built instantly is as fleeting as a beautiful sunset, unless you learn quickly to handle it. As evidenced by the many poverty-ridden lottery winners, this doesn't always happen. This is despite the fact that about forty percent of people are hoping to get lucky by hitting the lottery, winning a sweepstakes, getting an inheritance, or through marriage.

But hope without action is just an idea.

To create the future you want, you'll have to live for tomorrow and not just today. In our culture of immediate gratification and short attention spans, the future isn't sexy. Give me mine today. Instant fame, instant money, instant life. They can all vanish in an instant as well. Instead of wanting everything right now, allow things to mature and come in a way that is sustainable. Be willing to put off gratification.

One of my coaches told me, "Before you can become a millionaire, you have to learn to think like one". Before you can reach the level of having seven figures, you have to change your thinking again, and this continual reframing of your thinking repeats for each income level you try to reach.

However, if you are not earning six figures, you won't be ready for seven figures. You would be more likely to become one of the statistical sad stories of rags to riches to rags. There's a reason lottery winners who had nothing go right back to nothing. Their net worth changed, but not their mindset.

I want your success and your financial security to be lasting. Through this book, I can show you how and when you apply these skills, it'll mean more freedom for you. You'll be able to pay it forward with your knowledge and an example to family, friends, your community, and future generations.

Understanding Net Worth

Too many people aren't calculating a positive net worth, whether it's in liquid assets or tied up in real estate. In 2023, the average consumer debt was $104,000 according to Experian, a consumer credit agency.

This is a combination of car loans, credit cards, student loans, and mortgage debt. Mortgages were seventy percent of that debt, and consumer debt peaked in the fourth quarter of 2024.

If you'd like to see more data on consumer debt, visit the article here: https://www.fool.com/money/research/average-household-debt/.

***

Net Worth – Example

Net worth is what you have in value after subtracting anything you owe. So if you have $250,000 in the bank but owe $125,000 on your home (worth $125,000), $25,000 in student loans, $15,000 on your car, and $10,000 in consumer debt that you're carrying over from month to month, then your net worth is $75,000 ($250,000 minus the house, student loans, car, and consumer debt).

If you have $50,000 in the bank, owe $25,000 on a home worth $300,000, and have a $10,000 car loan, you have a net worth of $315,000. The person with $250,000 in the bank is more liquid (can more easily access their money) even though their overall net worth is lower.

***

The economy and people's financial pains have been a driving force behind political divisions and decisions in the United States. Anyone saying money doesn't matter is telling a flat-out lie. Money isn't the only solution to troubles, but it is a major one. It makes the hard times easier and the easy times sweeter.

For our financial goals, it took time and patience. We sacrificed and made choices that supported our goals for ourselves and our family. There's a good chance that if you truly want the transformation of having more abundance, you'll need to do the same.

We can do hard things now, so we can have it easier later, or take it easy now and have it harder later. The hard will be there at some point, but the more you follow what I share in this book, the less you'll feel like you're sacrificing. You'll see that you're investing in the only asset that is truly ever yours. Yourself. And if you happen to have children, you're also investing in their future.

Understanding ourselves and our relationship with money can help us stay ahead of behaviors that won't help us get where we want to go. So, what does it mean to be intentional about creating financial security and moving towards a rich life?

Be Intentional

On television, the rich are always dressed to the nines, driving luxurious cars, and living in multi-million-dollar homes. This is especially true on lifestyle television shows and movies. These people are not dressing like your everyday wealthy people. They're dressing like *very* wealthy people. There's a difference.

If you don't have to work, worry about a mortgage, college loans, college tuition, a car, or other things that most people consider, then spending what amounts to a car note or mortgage on a handbag or pair of shoes won't hurt you. If you are trying to become financially secure and even set yourself up to build wealth and become financially free, those types of purchases will keep you right where you are – under the illusion that you're trying.

In the early 1990s, I had the good fortune of attending school in one of the wealthiest school districts in the United States of America. We lived on the edge of the district in a very working-class town. I can recall going to school and seeing the rich kids wearing the same jeans they'd worn earlier that week.

There was no fashion show happening at Fox Chapel, though I'm sure the brand of t-shirts for some students cost more than for other students. But it was never a big deal or a focus point. Nobody cared! Their money went to other places.

Think about your purchases from a perspective of value and your financial goals.

This isn't to say you can't have fun. You can. But you can't have all the fun, all the time. Pick your non-negotiables and let yourself indulge in that thing within reason; unless that one thing will cause you not to reach your goals, no matter how much you cut elsewhere.

Being intentional also means being active in creating the life you want. We'll get into action in chapter nine, but as you read this book, keep it in the back of your mind that nothing will come of your reading this if you aren't taking intentional action. Put the skills to use. Practice what you learn in your life, even if you start with small actions. They build up over time.

Live With Your Priorities in Mind

As we built our wealth, we lived in average homes. It was only once we'd hit a level where we could buy the next home in cash that we bought a more luxurious home. We've invested in real estate for many years. We'd had very good returns on private equity investments, stocks, real estate investments, and equity in the home we'd owned since 2005. This, in addition to earned income, meant we were able to create a debt-free life.

If home ownership is a goal of yours, follow the market, look at non-traditional means of purchasing a home, such as through auctions or for-sale-by-owner, where you can save thousands of dollars. Just be sure to pay attention that the home prices, even if discounted, aren't overpriced. If you are reading this and home prices have peaked, be patient. It may take time for home prices to become more in line with incomes again.

While waiting for the market to rebalance and for prices to come down, consider saving your money towards a down payment. At the same time, ensure your credit profile is strong so you can buy your home with the best possible terms. We'll cover credit and debt in chapter six.

Living Within Your Vision

In November 2016, I bought a Chrysler Town & Country minivan. At the time, my kids were fourteen and four, and I'd vowed right up until they dragged me into a minivan on the dealership lot that I would never be a minivan mom. Eight years later, I was still driving Bessie. It was only when I could purchase my next car in cash and get a great deal that I went for a used, low-mileage Mercedes.

As a Saver money mojo type with a strong secondary Seeker type, this wasn't that hard for me to do. Stars and Spenders may have a harder time delaying that gratification, but choosing to live within your vision means making choices that support your future self. You can find out your Money Mojo type by taking my free quiz at BernetteSherman.com/quiz.

As for this Saver, I plan on driving her until my next milestone birthday! My husband, as the President of a company, drove a Honda Fit for years until our daughter got her license and he upgraded his vehicle, again paying in cash.

Can you be okay not keeping up with the Joneses? Especially since the Joneses are probably in more debt than they would ever admit.

As a family, we prioritize the things we care about. Vacations and experiences are something we prioritize as a couple and family. For example, we could spend more than

$5,000 a year on car notes for one vehicle or drive a car well past its being paid for and go on nice vacations each year. Seeing interesting places around the world is part of our vision for a rich life.

Making sure our kids have college funds and can participate in extracurricular activities comes ahead of other possible purchases and expenses. I spend a lot on food every month, but choosing healthier options for my family is a priority for me. Remember what I said about money being able to afford you better options and better health? This is one example.

When the economy turns south and we're faced with higher costs and stagnant wages, many struggle to pay for their basic living expenses, including paying for housing and food, let alone living below their means. When basic necessities take up more than their fair share of income, it's hard to feel as if you can get ahead and build a path to a life that feels rich.

If you are seeking to build a richer life with freedom and more enjoyment, but are not meeting your basic human needs, pause. Take care of your basic needs first. Use the tools I share in this book and my *Money Mojo Workbook* and apply them to getting a higher-paying position or a raise, improving your credit profile, paying off and lowering debt, or reducing expenses while increasing income where possible. *This comes first.* Otherwise, you'll have a hard time getting to the next financial level because you won't have the mindset to get there and stay there.

How well you do this might be impacted by your money mojo style and your approach to money. Taking the quiz will give you more perspective on some of your personal behaviors and attitudes about money. It can be very helpful when you are faced with challenges in the areas of saving, spending, credit, debt management, and even going after your financial dreams.

This quiz will tell you which of the five money mojo types you most strongly identify with, as well as your secondary type or types. The five money mojo types are Saver, Spender, Servant, Seeker, and Saver. Each relates to money in slightly different ways. The details of each type are available to you when you complete the quiz.

When you understand your money mojo, which goes beyond the money mojo type, and learn to shift it where needed, you can create a healthier, more fulfilling relationship with money. This can often free you up energetically to expand in other areas, without financial stressors.

I like the idea of imagining you are free from limiting beliefs, with more self-awareness, and ultimately, living a life that is in line with your values, priorities, and dreams. That's what I call a rich life.

Your Values and Vision

Before moving forward in this book, ask yourself a few questions. These questions are also in the *Money Mojo Workbook*; however, the workbook does have the complete list of questions as well as ideas for brainstorming your values.

Our thoughts and actions have to be aligned in order for us to be successful. This is where mindset comes into play. If there is a part of you that doesn't believe you can get out of debt, save money, have a secure future, or create wealth, then your mind will have to prove itself right - and you won't.

In order to have the lifestyle you want, you have to believe it's possible.

I grew up without much in the way of money. I was raised by a single mom, and we spent my childhood in lower-income housing. But my mom had a plan for us. Go to college so we could get out and have a better life. All three of us did just that, creating lives of abundance, travel, and financial security for our families. We all used our degrees and did other things to create income, such as investing and real estate.

You don't have to be born into money to start creating financial security and prosperity. If you want it and are willing to do the work to have it, it can be yours too.

Values

Everyone has values and priorities that impact how they live and the decisions they make in the short-term and the long-term. Your values often drive you at a deeper level, while priorities may shift based on your current situation.

What's important to you?

Consider these high-level areas. Take the time to think through these areas and write down any thoughts you have around the terms here. Write down the values you hold in each of them.

- Integrity & Ethics
- Growth and Learning
- Relationships and Connection
- Well-being and Fulfillment
- Achievement and Contribution
- Personal Qualities and Traits
- Freedom and Autonomy
- Anything else like traditions, security, freedom

Your values shape how you show up in the world and how you relate to others. They will impact the vision you cast as well.

Vision

Your vision is personal, non-transferable, dynamic, felt, and seen. It will focus on the future and should inspire you and stretch you at the same time.

You can choose to have a written vision statement for your life paired with one you quite literally visualize. I think they are most powerful when you pair the two together, allowing the written one, which can be spoken, to serve as a tool to call up the mental image of the life you want to create.

Many people use vision boards to help them visualize their goals and ideal lifestyle. However, you can also keep it in your mind or combine all of these methods.

The written ones should be easy to memorize so you can quickly recall them to recenter, repeating them as you need to whenever you feel yourself getting off course.

Your vision statement can be used as part of prayers and meditations on a daily basis to keep you focused on your target. Use your visualization whenever you have free time to let your mind wander to the reality you are creating.

What's your financial vision for your life?

What goals do you have for your financial future?

What does having a rich and abundant life mean to you?

If you are in a relationship, have the vision and goals been decided by and agreed on by both of you?

Chapter Three

A Rich Life for Couples

When it comes to money, both people in a relationship need to commit to shared goals. You don't need to have *exactly* the same individual aspirations, but your big financial vision should be aligned.

Without a shared vision, you'll find yourselves constantly at odds, pulling in different directions instead of working together to build a life you both truly desire. Your financial harmony isn't just about spreadsheets; it's about building a shared future.

Look at the goals you've come up with as more than just dollar figures. Then ask yourself some questions, together.

- What do these aspirations *mean* for your family, for your life together, for the experiences you want to share? For example, does your dream of buying a home symbolize stability, a place to grow roots, or a legacy for your children? Does saving for travel mean creating cherished memories and expanding your horizons as a couple?

- Do your primary financial goals genuinely match up?
- Do you both agree on the life and lifestyle you want to create and the experiences you want to have as you build your rich life together?

Before moving forward, take the time to ensure you are truly on the same path; otherwise, you'll wind up moving in different directions, and that friction can wear down even the strongest relationships.

It may help to know your money mojo types before you sit down to discuss how you align and your goals.

Your Financial Partnership

It's not sexy or romantic, but marriage is a legal agreement between two people and was historically very much related to business. Cattle, livestock, and valuables were exchanged for a spouse, and families considered the value the other person brought to the partnership. This wasn't just monetary, but might be socially as well.

Your modern partnership still has some remnants of the historical element. If you aren't married, you won't get the tax benefits or benefits of being in a legally recognized relationship when it comes to important decisions such as healthcare. And committed relationships today come with other challenges and considerations. With most households having both parents working, it can be easy to just say split it evenly.

However, when it comes to saving and investing, if both of you work, consider agreeing on a percentage, not a fixed dollar amount, that each of you will consistently put into a joint savings or investment account. This creates more fairness and adaptability as incomes might change over time.

You may also want to have a clear agreement that neither of you will make withdrawals from that account without first discussing it thoroughly with each other. Discussing means more than sending a text that you're spending money from the savings account without allowing time for a conversation. This builds trust and prevents misunderstandings down the line.

Given that the number one reason for marriages to end is money or finances, having these conversations when there isn't an issue can prevent the tension when there is an issue with money.

Before you even start, set out in advance your shared goals for these funds, your collective risk tolerance (how much you can both comfortably handle when your balances or losses to up or down), and how you will manage any earnings from the account. Will you reinvest them to accelerate growth, or will some be earmarked for immediate shared enjoyment?

Having these conversations up front means there won't be conflict or confusion later because you've both agreed to the strategy.

While you're preparing for the future, set check-ins for your financial health and revisit the goals and decisions to make sure you are both still in agreement. You'll want to do this at least once a year, but if your finances are changing quickly, check in more frequently, and if you have a major life event change, revisit your financial vision and decisions.

Sometimes, reaching your financial goals as a couple might require one of you to invest significant time or money into furthering your education or career development. This is a topic that's absolutely worthy of deep discussion.

Talk about the potential impact, the sacrifices, and the long-term benefits for both of you. Remember, you're in this together. This isn't one person's burden; it's a shared investment in your collective future.

Relationships are partnerships, and that extends to your financial well-being. Hold each other accountable in a loving, kind, and supportive way. Speak to each other with the same respect and encouragement you'd want to receive.

Encourage each other to live in a way that honors your time, personal growth, and individual well-being. This might mean making space for a partner to pursue a hobby that refreshes them, even if it has a small cost, because their mental health benefits the partnership.

***

Alignment in Action, Case Study

Michael and Angela (not real names) came to me because they wanted to have a family, but knew they needed to get some of their financial business in order. Part of their vision for their family was that Michael would be the primary breadwinner while Angela took care of their home and the children they'd have.

When Angela reached out, it was because she was growing frustrated with their progress saving money and suspected it was because Michael was spending more than they'd budgeted for.

She'd told me that Michael grew up not having very much money. When he graduated from college and got a well-paying job, a part of him felt he needed to show his success. She said he'd always been generous with family and friends who needed help, even when he didn't really have the money.

When I spoke to him, he admitted that when he and his brothers went out, he would pick up the check. He sent a cousin money occasionally, usually out of a sense of obligation. He spent his money as fast as he made it because of always taking care of others.

As one of the oldest children in his family group, he had always helped out his younger siblings and cousins. That mindset was now costing his own happiness and financial security.

Before Angela and Michael could begin saving for their future together and the family they wanted to have, he knew he had to change this.

It took Michael a few months to unwind himself from always paying. He admitted it was difficult to say no. We finally came up with a solution so he could manage it more easily. He took cash only with him and knew how much he had available for his bill. When the check came, he paid cash.

He told me it was extremely uncomfortable the first time, since he didn't have a card on him. His brothers looked confused but were forced to pay for their own bills. He had to literally sit on his hands and bite the inside of his lip. He also said he realized he wasn't helping his brothers be more mature and responsible by always paying the bill.

He had always felt responsible for them since they didn't grow up with a father. He had to do a lot of work on revising his own money stories so he wouldn't feel guilty. Together, we set the goal of helping them become more financially capable, using the tools and skills they were learning by working together.

Angela's seeker type was a great support when it came to finding solutions for them to save their money. She found deals, a savings account that had a high yield interest rate, and sought out cheaper services for their utilities. It was fun to see her come alive in taking ownership of this.

They managed to save over fifty dollars a month just by changing some of their services. They used this money to pay off a credit card they had for furniture they purchased.

Money saved from not being responsible for everyone else saved Michael and Angela over two hundred dollars a month. That money went into their emergency fund. Once the credit card is paid off, that money will go into their home fund, towards their down payment, along with an extra fifty dollars Angela has budgeted from her paycheck.

In Michael and Angela's case, they didn't choose to increase their income yet as they were both working full-time, but chose to focus on reducing their expenses.

Angela keeps a close eye on other opportunities to save and helps Michael stay accountable to their goals by not overspending on family and friends.

Michael still likes to enjoy himself and go out, which he does. But instead of spending his money all the time, he's working on spending only on special occasions, like birthdays. It still lets him feel good and supportive without setting them back. For this, he puts twenty-five dollars each paycheck into his short-term account so when he needs to get a birthday gift or pay for the dessert, he can.

Michael and Angela's desire for a stable home and a place to build a future was their motivation to shift their mindsets, and now they are on the path to living both their values and vision for their family.

***

What Michael and Angela experienced isn't uncommon. Everyone comes into relationships with their own money ghost stories and patterns. Michael's patterns were impacting their ability to reach their goals, and though he was acting out of his sense of duty and responsibility, he wasn't aligned with the vision and values he and Angela had set as his primary responsibility.

As this is a money book to help you create a rich life, I will stick to that aspect. Choosing to co-create a life of abundance, security, and enjoyment with a partner will take patience, kindness, and plenty of communication. Together, you get to choose what that looks like and align your choices and actions with the vision you've set.

Chapter Four

Why You Need Money Skills

Many people won't talk about money. Not in the way we need to. Because of this, most people don't have the skills to handle the fundamentals, such as creating and using a budget, managing their credit and debt, and saving money. Without these basic areas under control, it will be impossible to build wealth or a secure financial future.

Don't believe that more money will solve it. There are plenty of stories of people who make a lot of money and are still living paycheck to paycheck or who have to file for bankruptcy. Michael and Angela made enough money to have savings, but spent more than they made.

There are plenty of famous people and celebrities who have experienced this too. Did you know Kim Basinger filed for bankruptcy in the past? She had a failed investment in Braselton, Georgia, as well as legal battles.

Mike Tyson earned more than 400 million dollars during his career. It seems enough to last anyone a lifetime. However, in 2003, he filed for bankruptcy due to overspending.

Other stars like Johnny Depp lost hundreds of millions of dollars due to financial mismanagement and overspending. He had a penchant for homes, art, and wine. And if you're my age, you remember MC Hammer. Made famous in the 1990s, he was bankrupt by 1996 from excessive spending, despite having made millions of dollars.

The idea that the rich and famous don't have money problems is false. If you don't know how to manage your money and have ghost stories about money, it'll follow you wherever you are.

Getting the fundamentals in order sets the foundation you'll build on. Remember what I said about doing the harder things now? Some of this may seem hard, but it can make the future easier. This is especially true when you can live without the weight of debt, meet your basic living expenses, enjoy life, and have money for the future.

All of the people I mentioned above successfully made a lot of money. That's something not everyone manages to do. However, they also successfully lost a lot of money. Using the skills you'll learn in this book, you can avoid that pitfall. Why? Because when we know better, we can do better.

When I first started college, I was excited to fill out a credit card form for Macy's on campus. They were going to give me a $500 credit limit to buy whatever I wanted from Macy's based on my student status and income from my student work-study job.

What they failed to tell me and what I didn't know was that the bill would be due every month, with a minimum payment, and interest accruing, and sky-high interest rates if I missed a payment. Which I did!

They didn't mention that it would go on my credit report and sit there for years, when I didn't even understand what a credit report was. I barely understood what 'run your credit' meant, especially since at eighteen, I didn't have any, and in my home, the most I remember us having was debit cards.

They must've been the same, right? Wrong. Oh, was I wrong, and I paid for that lack of knowledge halfway through my twenties.

When I moved from the apartment I'd been living in, I didn't change my mailing address for Macy's and stopped receiving the bills. It was out of sight, out of mind. Only when I went in to purchase something did I learn that I had a balance of over $700!

I'd been charged interest and late fees to the point that, even though I'd previously made payments, all of that was wiped away. I was more in debt than when I'd bought those two leather coats. One of which I wore for more than a decade because I'd paid so much for it!

When we don't have the knowledge, we can find ourselves in situations that cost us. In another situation, I lost my job just a few months after purchasing a home. While I wasn't aware of it at the time, I was one of the many who experienced the dot com bubble burst. I was just twenty-four years old, and while I'd managed to buy a home, I still had a lot to learn.

In desperation, I cashed a check that was an offer for a personal loan. It was over $2,000, which meant it could help with mortgage and bills while I continued to look for a job. It had come in the mail at what seemed like just the right time. Money was getting tight, and the economy had slowed.

Did I read the fine print? Yes, I did. Did I fully appreciate what it meant when it said that the interest rate was double-digits and missing payments would increase it? Maybe not close enough.

Soon, I found myself not just paying for student loans, a mortgage, a car note, insurance, and other household bills, but now there was this extra debt payment along with that Macy's card, a card from Sears, and a couple of other small lines of credit. I had bitten off more than I could chew, even with finally getting a job six months after being let go.

Before I knew it, I was pushing back the payment dates, making smaller payments, and on occasion, I was paying right at the last moment. There were plenty of months when I would drive my car to the bank that had financed my car loan to pay them the day it was due.

At the time, I was married to someone who is now my ex-husband. Neither of us had good money skills or money sense. We'd both grown up in low-income households where there wasn't much access to credit or income, so we hadn't learned to manage our money well. See the chapter for couples on some important tips and lessons for working in a partnership to become financially secure.

As a young adult, I had no thoughts about saving money, retirement, or financial security. We were pretty much living paycheck to paycheck with a little available if something needed to be repaired or replaced, but nothing for the future. I thought the retirement contribution being taken out through the university I worked for was enough.

Clearly, I wasn't a math major, because there was no way that was going to secure my future. And once I became a mom, it was even more important that I became responsible because an entire other human being was now relying on us.

One of my first actions in getting my life together was choosing to be single. I decided that it was better to be single than to have the marriage I was in be the model of a relationship for my daughter.

I never wanted her to think she was a second-class person because she was a girl or woman, or meant to be subservient for those reasons. Before having my daughter I'd already begun to see my life in a different way.

I'd started to change as a person and in my beliefs. There was a remembering of what was possible for me and the person I really was, and not who I'd allowed myself to believe I was.

I got intentional about my life and the quality of life I wanted for myself and my daughter. When I chose to leave that unhealthy marriage, I was forced to sit down and make a budget.

I was afraid I wouldn't be able to make it on my own, but doing the budget, understanding my income, expenses, and then what I could afford to do gave me the power to make decisions for the future I was intentionally creating.

Whatever your reasons, getting your money fundamentals in order will give you a sense of power that you can use to intentionally create the life you want. Whether it is just for yourself, for your family, or to be of higher service in your community.

What It Means to Be Intentional About Your Finances

Being intentional about your financial security means taking an honest look at your finances by knowing your numbers and then taking actions that align with your financial goals.

These numbers include your current income and earnings from all sources, your current and regular expenditures for the month and the year, your level of debt and the cost of that debt and repayment terms, your current savings, and the expected cost of planned purchases.

Knowing your numbers gives you a kind of dashboard for your financial health. You can do a monthly checkup using these numbers along with the benchmarks you set. A college student used the tools and skills I share in this book to purchase his car debt-free. Was it a new and fancy car? No. Was it one that could get him to school and work so he could invest in himself and his future? Absolutely!

This book is to help you develop practical money skills to improve your financial wellness and increase your financial security. You'll get principles in core personal finance areas, along with some of my insights from lived experiences and clients I've worked with.

By the end, you'll have the tools to shift your money skills. *Money Skills for Your Rich Life* covers the following topics:

Income and Earnings

- Savings, expenses, and budgeting
- Debt and loans
- Account management
- Credit
- Basic investing

You may also want to consider educating yourself on economic and government influences, risk management and insurance, and retirement planning.

Chapter Five

Income and Earnings

To feel prosperous and build a life of financial security and freedom, you need money coming in. While we can talk all day about changing your mindset and behaviors around money, how it actually enters your life can't be ignored. Money allows you to pay down the debt you may have accumulated and to begin saving money to fuel your future goals.

The main goal of having a job or career is to make money to live the lifestyle you want now and to plan for a comfortable future. But work can be more than just making money. We spend about one-third of our lives working. That's about roughly 100,000 hours.

Finding work that genuinely resonates with you, work that aligns with your deeper purpose, isn't just about financial health. It's about your overall well-being and how long you live.

If you find your income isn't covering your needs, your goals for saving, and your everyday living expenses, you have two options: reduce expenses or increase income. Brainstorming income-making ideas is a smart move. Think about side hustles, gig work, a part-time job, or even asking for more hours or a pay raise at your current job. These are all real possibilities.

If you like your current job or career, how can you earn more there? Can you upskill and improve your knowledge or abilities to make yourself more valuable? This matters whether you plan to stay put or just want to be more competitive in the job market.

For those employed, consider talking to your manager about extra hours or a raise. Many people don't ask, so they don't get. When you do approach your manager, be ready to make your case by showing how you have been a benefit to the company and contribute to the bottom line.

Now, if your workplace is already cutting back, reducing staff, or showing other signs of financial struggles, you should be actively researching other opportunities, figuring out any knowledge or skill gaps you have, and filling them. Don't wait until you've been handed a pink slip or sent a text that you've been terminated to prepare for your next position.

It's my advice that you have the next position lined up before quitting a job that is stable and secure. Stability includes more than just a stable company, but you also need to be stable in your position. If you're in a job that is causing more than normal levels of stress and affecting your mental health, that job isn't stable. However, before quitting and facing the additional stress of mounting bills and a lack of income, create a plan for your exit.

One thing I've learned in the many jobs I've had over the years is that it is important to leave professionally and properly. I've left jobs professionally and then been asked to take on both short-term and long-term consulting roles, because not only did I do a good job while there, but I left on good terms.

I believe that how you leave one thing is how you enter the next thing. Leave on good terms so that energy follows you to the next opportunity.

In the *Money Mojo Workbook*, I've got a section on Income for brainstorming ideas, evaluating them, and creating your plan. In today's economy, side hustles and gig work are common ways to earn extra cash. They don't have to be permanent, especially if your goals are short-term, like paying off debt or saving for a trip or a concert.

The more you can avoid debt or loans by having enough income to support your lifestyle, the better off you'll be long-term.

Identify Work That Aligns With Your Purpose

How do you find work that truly connects with your purpose and values? It starts with looking inward. Many of us haven't really taken the time to dig into what kind of work aligns with our deepest beliefs.

Think of it like this: your skills, interests, and even the problems that keep you up at night aren't just random facts about you. They're clues to what you could be doing for income. Get out a notebook or some paper and ask yourself some questions to start thinking about what inspires and moves you at a deeper level.

- What are you naturally good at?
- What skills have you developed over the years?
- What do people come to you for or ask you for help with?
- What do you do in your free time?
- What issues in the world or in your community keep you up at night?

- What subjects can you lose yourself in?
- What subjects could you be a forever-student of?

Once you've identified these insights, look at them through an income lens. What do people often ask you for help with, or what do you love doing that others find valuable? We often give these "gifts" away for free. That's fine if you don't need more income, but if you do, these are excellent starting points.

You can test the waters by offering your skill to a few clients, get their feedback, refine your offering, and then figure out your costs and profit before offering it again.

If you're already doing a side hustle or gig, see where you're at with it using the conscious savings and spending plan concept discussed in the next chapter, and apply it to your business. Where can you cut expenses to boost your take-home pay from it? If it's not making money, what changes can you make to earn more from the effort you're already putting in?

Create Your Desired Work Life

Once you know the kind of work that truly aligns with you, it's time to figure out how to make it your living. This might mean pursuing a specific job or creating your own path by starting a business.

If you're goal is a traditional job, start by researching online and networking with people in your desired field. Go after those opportunities, and if you need more skills or certifications, get them through courses or classes. There are online and in-person options for many topics, and some resources may even be free. Do your homework.

If you're thinking about working for yourself, many resources can help you start a business. For freelance work, explore online platforms that connect clients with independent professionals. You can build your portfolio by taking on initial projects for friends or family. Starting this way lets you test your concept before expanding to a larger audience.

Build your network by reaching out to professionals on networking sites like LinkedIn or connecting through your local Chamber of Commerce, Rotary Club, or other associations.

You might consider networking with those in your faith community, kids' sports teams, your gym, and your alma mater, or that of other colleges and universities in your area. When you register, you'll find out if it's open to the public and whether events are focused on a particular industry.

If you are an entrepreneur, creative, sell products, or do anything else independently, creating supportive and networks where there is mutual benefit is important.

Whether you want a traditional career or to be independently employed, don't overlook local support. Look into professional associations, free business mentors often available through community organizations, or local groups that share your interests.

Have A Path to Income

If you are planning to make a transition that requires reeducation, what will you do to earn extra income between now and getting the additional education and skills you need? How will you pay for the education, tools, or additional skills?

It's important to budget this into your conscious savings and spending plan before enrolling and incurring additional student loans or personal debt. Before enrolling in an educational program do research on the job forecast for the career you are pursuing, what the earning potential is in your area, and how competitive it is.

Are there many jobs or is it the type of field where only one or two positions in an entire state are available? If you're planning to learn a trade, does the school help with on the job training and work placement? Does it have a good track record and proof of students graduating and working?

If you need to earn income while upskilling, consider the skills you already have that you can use for side gigs and extra money. Revisit the ideas above about earning extra income and managing your conscious savings and spending plan so you minimize the amount of future debt obligations you have.

Be Willing to Learn and Grow

Inside every great leader is a great follower. Inside every great teacher is a great student. A thirst for knowledge and learning is essential to building wealth. Whether it's a general love of learning or specific to the area you are most interested in, be open and curious.

I believe we are here on this planet to have life abundantly, to interact with others, to learn, and to grow. And growth is essential. When we're open to being taught by those who know more than us, we do two things. We allow someone else to interact with us, to share themselves, and to be useful and valuable. We also share ourselves with someone else and learn new things.

If we aren't growing, we're dying. It's the nature of life. Just as with how we nourish our bodies, if we don't nourish our minds we will be malnourished and begin to decline.

As long as we allow ourselves to learn new things and think new thoughts, we allow ourselves to grow in new ways. Otherwise, we become stagnant and eventually the opposite becomes true.

How's that beer commercial go? 'Stay thirsty, my friends.'

During the summer leading up my seventh grade year, as a gangly twelve-year-old, my family moved from a small town in South Carolina to the Fox Chapel school district. Based on my grades and placement from before, I was put in the accelerated reading class.

I was in a bit of culture shock (which I won't go into here) and trying to adjust. At the end of the first grading period, I distinctly remember the teacher pointing out the paper she'd tacked to the wall. It had the names of all of the honor roll students. My stomach sank. I wasn't on the list.

She then went on to say that if you were in that class, accelerated reading, you should be on the list. I'd narrowly missed that 3.0, but after that, I was on the honor roll for the rest of my school years, except for one quarter in college. Business calculus kicked my behind.

In Pittsburgh, I had friends who ran the spectrum. I saw the difference between my friends who had upper-middle-class to upper class families and those who were lower-middle-class to poor. There were also differences in opportunity and access.

Education isn't important because it somehow shows you're smarter. It's important because it means you are teachable and willing to learn. Higher education might also show that you have commitment and perseverance and can complete your goals.

Many things have changed with education since that time, and some might argue that our current system doesn't prepare our children for the real world and college is no longer affordable. To that, I can't argue. But, education is still important. Whatever it is you want to do, be willing to learn how to do it. Winging it and learning on the fly, while it may seem cool, will cost you both time and money.

How you learn doesn't have to follow tradition. For example, learning from an expert or someone doing what you want to do can be much more effective than learning from a classroom teacher on the theory of doing what you want to do.

Trades and hands-on skills are just as important as STEM careers. There is a place for the arts, though we always need more financial support for the arts so that creative and regular performing artists can live.

It is possible to work within the system while continuing to expand yourself outside of the system. The system is just another tool. Use it as best you can while making sure your needs to learn what you want to learn are met.

If you're reading this and have children, I hope you'll let the prior paragraphs soak in a bit. If you're reading this as an adult who has already gotten past your formal education, it doesn't mean your learning is done and you can't get additional education to increase your opportunities to manifest money.

If you're in a field that has the potential to earn you a strong income but you can't seem to break through, it means you could benefit from learning something new either through training, workshops, seminars, or a successful mentor.

The keys I share with you can work when you have a vehicle for the money to flow through. Some vehicles have more space to carry your growing wealth. As you open yourself to learning and growth, consider which paths allow you to funnel more money into your life.

A brief aside. I am personally leery of the wave of coaches and gurus selling courses to teach you how to be a coach like them. I think it's the new multi-level-marketing plan but now you don't even get a real product. Please be careful before signing up to a course where the creator doesn't have a history of success other than selling courses. Okay, back to it.

If you need to change fields so that you can have a better chance of earning more, now is the time to prepare yourself for the change.

Invest in Yourself

As adults, we're pretty much on our own. If you want it, you have to be willing to do it. The investment may be of your time, your talent, or your treasure (money).

For example, if you dream of being a writer (like I did) you will have to invest your time to write and to develop your skills and your treasure to actually publish quality material. While I have decided to put down the pen on fiction, I've authored and published more than a dozen books including novels, poetry, self-help, and inspirational books.

I've invested a significant amount of time in the actual process of writing out the stories, learning the craft of self-publishing, finding the right help for everything from covers to editing, and so much more. But, it was an investment in myself that I truly value. With each publication it got easier. The knowledge became mine.

If you want to run your own business, you first need to learn about the business you want to start. Whatever it is, study it, talk to professionals in the field, visit the websites of existing businesses. If they have a physical location, visit those too. Join online forums or networking groups for people who are in that line of work. Be willing to listen to those who have knowledge either from experience or from formal education.

If being an entrepreneur is the path you are on or want to be on, I encourage you to get a business coach who has lived experience so they can help you avoid pitfalls.

You don't need to have a business or be an entrepreneur to create wealth. You can also be an intrapreneur or simply involve yourself in a side hustle. Our primary wealth was built from my husband's traditional career along with real estate investing. My books didn't pay any real bills but they were my personal creative outlet and manifestation tools.

The investment of time can't be underestimated when it comes to creating a wealth and prosperity mindset. If you are willing to invest time and energy into something that you love and the world needs and values, you'll see the rewards.

A warning: Many people allow this to become an excuse. Over-learning, over-investigating, and under-acting. We need balance. Learn, do, grow. Learn what you need to get started. Do what you've learned. Grow from what you do. Learn more to do more to grow more. Learning and growth are an endless part of the cycle. Learning by itself yields little. You must implement what you learn.

Returning to school, learning a trade, or even attending a conference can sometimes feel burdensome. Figure out if the return on the investment, long-term and short-term, will help you move closer to your goals. Not every educational opportunity will pass the test and you should weigh the cost of the opportunity, any financing costs, and loss of current wages with opportunities for advancement, new earnings, and other benefits.

If you are interested in returning to college, consider finding a job with a company that offers tuition reimbursement. It may require being employed there for a certain period of time before getting the benefit, but could end up saving you thousands while you're still earning an income.

I earned my Masters in Public Administration while employed full-time at Georgia State University. I graduated without having to pay for anything besides books and general materials. Once I finished, my salary increased because I had an advanced degree.

Recently, I wanted to invest in coaching and personal development for myself but I personally wasn't earning enough to cover the high investment. I returned to work so I could have my own personal income, not just our joint earnings, to invest in myself. Yes, even though we have more income and wealth than most, I went back to work temporarily to achieve certain goals.

Prioritize what's important for you when considering how you'll invest in yourself to take yourself to the next level. How can the investment open up new doors and opportunities?

Money Containers

Before starting this section, I must say that I am not a wealth advisor or a financial advisor. I am a Certified Financial Education Instructor, and I happen to be a manifestor who has successfully manifested money.

Any information in this book, in part or in total, is based on our personal experiences and cannot be taken as professional advice. I assume no liability for how you choose to apply any of this information and simply share what has worked for us.

Many people who desire financial security, freedom, and flexibility choose to go the entrepreneurial route. I get it, I've leaned into it myself. I've leaned back from it too, at times, choosing instead to shape how I serve others around my ideal lifestyle. However, that's not how we wound up where we are financially.

Creating abundance in the form of money can come in many ways. It's not just what flows into your household, but what doesn't flow out. You can think of it like pipes. Water is always able to run through your pipes. When you turn on the faucet, it comes out. If there is nothing for the water to pour into, it just goes back into the drain for recirculation.

However, if you have a container to catch it, you can start accumulating more currency. On the other hand, if your faucet is leaky or your pipes are leaking, you are losing the water before you even have a chance to put it to use.

Let's keep going with this container idea. The currency we are talking about here is money. If we remove a container, money can't flow into it, but it can flow into a different container. If there are no containers whatsoever, you're missing out on all of that potential. Get some containers!

You cannot bring money into your life and hold onto it if you don't have a container to catch it. For example, someone without a container will rely on friends and family loaning them money, and that money won't be something they can hold. It'll be used immediately to meet needs and then have to be repaid.

Payday loans, buy now pay later loans, and other borrowing, like credit cards, will be even worse. It's like having a container with a large hole in it. The money flows in, but you don't get the full benefit because it's going to cost you more than you received.

Growing up, we didn't talk much about money, except that we didn't have it and were broke. I remember being a young adult, counting every single penny to make sure I had enough to get through the week or month. This meant I had to get comfortable with money and getting into the details. It's a responsibility that my husband and I share.

If you need to pay down debt, focus on this first. And yes, with good money mojo, you can create and find extra resources to pay off debt or have it erased. You can receive bonuses, gifts, and surprise money in the mail with the intention of getting rid of debt. When it comes, remember the goal. Pay down your debt so you can become debt-free.

If you can start saving, begin putting money into a savings account that pays interest. Shop around for accounts that pay higher interest and that don't charge fees. If you've done that truth moment by looking at your real money situation, you know what you have coming in, going out, and what you can be flexible with. It doesn't matter how much that amount is, as long as it's positive. Trust me.

This is an exercise in being intentional with your actions. If you want to start saving so you can start investing or reaching other financial goals, do this, whether you have ten cents left over or one hundred dollars.

You've probably heard the concept of having envelopes or buckets of money. The envelope method is one I used with Michael and Angela. With this method, some envelopes are literal envelopes and some are used only to portion out your money before putting it into an account or taking some other useful action.

Let's use the theme of envelopes, which you fill from the money you collect in your containers. You would have an envelope that you designate for different parts of your budget, once bills are paid.

Ramit Sethi doesn't suggest creating a budget, and neither do I. We do have a conscious savings and spending plan, and there are some things that are important to us, like experiences and travel, and other things that aren't important to us, like fashion or having the trendiest…anything.

One of the key things here is that you know what your priorities are and the things that make your life feel special. I like to travel and enjoy good food and museums. This means we are willing to spend more for those things, but you better believe I'm checking all the prices when I'm buying clothes and anything else. As a Saver money mojo type, it's just what I do. It wouldn't hurt for other money mojo types to do it as well.

With groceries, I mentioned that we spend a lot on food because it is important, so yes, I like to buy good and wholesome food most of the time. However, I also clip coupons in the app and stock up on items we use often if they are on sale.

Again, I am a Saver. If your Money Mojo type is a Spender, you're not looking so closely at the prices and are buying what you want, sometimes even if it's not something you can afford.

Guilt or shame isn't part of being a conscious creator of a great financial future. This book isn't on conscious creation or manifestation, but whether you are the one creating your financial reality.

A mindset that has you feeling shame or guilt will absolutely change what you create. If you are conscientious about having more money to reach your goals and you have an envelope for fun money that you add to, based on your predefined percentages or amounts, and then you use it for fun, don't feel guilty!

Let me give you an example of what this might look like on shoestring finances. Say you have ten dollars left at the end of paying your bills each month. You may decide to have five main envelopes of Pay Down Debt, Savings (long-term savings), Emergency, Fun (short-term savings), and Kids stuff (a subdivided bucket of short-term savings).

You may then decide that the priority is paying down your debt, so you are giving that envelope half of everything you have left over. Five dollars goes into the Pay Down Debt envelope. Your Savings and Emergency envelopes are also important for you, but you realize that until you pay down your debt, saving money isn't as much of a priority, so you decide to put thirty percent of what's left in your Emergency envelope.

You've got twenty percent left over for Fun and Kids. Anyone with children knows something is going to come up unexpectedly. What do you mean the field trip is next week, and the money is due tomorrow? When did you get this permission slip? And of course, the answer to that question is a sheepish shrug or a vague mumble of an answer.

So, if you're a parent, you're putting ten percent or a dollar into the Kids container. No kids? Put that money into the best bucket to help you reach your goals. You have ten percent left for Fun, which means you've got one dollar in your Fun container.

Now, I know what you're thinking. In this economy, what are you doing for fun with a buck? You're adding to it and looking forward to your goal with some delayed gratification.

See, there's this thing I mentioned earlier. You can do hard now or hard later. But hard later is harder than hard now. Delaying gratification and having something to look forward to can keep you motivated.

Maybe you know you want to be able to treat yourself to a delicious chocolate chip cookie at a local bakery you pass by. The smell titillates your senses, leaving you with dreams of dunking that cookie in a glass of lactose-free milk. Hold that thought. Put the money in the envelope (in the form of a savings account) and watch your money grow.

This all works together. When you start putting everything in this little book together with general positive mindset principles, each envelope grows faster. It's like you turn on the faucet on a higher setting.

While this book isn't about manifestation or conscious creation, I want to share this experience with you briefly. If you are in a situation of trying to become financially secure, it may be helpful to consider how you might apply this in your life. Recently, I experimented with a money manifestation song I wrote and was singing around the house to manifest some money into our lives.

Within six weeks, a contract worth over $40,000 came through our business, and we got a multi-six-figure opportunity out of the blue through my husband. I joked that I didn't care how silly I looked singing and dancing to my money song. It did the job, and we had a money container available to receive the flow.

We've also gotten returns higher than average on investments and real estate by following my intuition. On the flip side, we've saved money by doing the same thing.

You can use the tactics here to start turning the financial tide in your home and really seeing the power you hold over your choices, even if they feel small now. How we handle the small things will allow us to better handle the big things when they come up.

Our Money Containers

What worked for us, may not work for you, and the speed at which the economy and technology are changing, career paths that were popular ten years ago are vanishing. I won't go into how we made all of our money since I do like my privacy, but I will share how we made some of our money.

Corporate Career

When we got married, we both worked full time in more traditional jobs. I, at a university working in community and public health research, and he in a corporate position. As I stepped back from my traditional career, my husband stepped forward. By caring for our home, he was able to really lean in, and I had the mental space to take care of the home without the worry of also taking care of bills.

Taking care of the home is more than doing laundry and cleaning; it's also taking care of the spiritual and emotional needs of the household and the house. Because I was holding that energetic space and ensuring the home ran smoothly, he could focus on his career, advancing into top C-suite positions.

However, for a period of two and a half years, I did return to work for a couple of reasons. One, I needed something I felt was productive. This was when I still felt like my work in the home wasn't enough. Yes, despite now realizing the powerful purpose I hold in my primary role, I didn't fully appreciate it until Covid hit.

The second reason was to generate investment income. The money I earned, I funneled into investments in myself and in passive real estate opportunities, allowing us to further advance financially. It also allowed us to avoid and eliminate debt by focusing the use of that income long-term to benefit us long-term.

When I left that job a year into Covid, I had what I needed, had met the goals I'd set out to reach with money, and was able to return my energy to my primary role as an Ama de Casa while continuing my work as a creative, coach, and mentor. I was able to be creative, flexible, and work on my terms.

This is the path we've chosen based on our priorities and the options available to us. You do what's most aligned with you. If you wish to be a stay-at-home partner, evaluate what options you have, what choices you'll need to make, and determine if it's possible.

Real Estate Investing

When we got married, I had a rental property that I rented out for more than fifteen years before selling it at a profit. For a while, we also rented out the home we bought together when we married, allowing equity to build back up after the 2008 global financial crisis. We sold that property with sizeable profits in 2023.

Between 2005 and now, we've also invested in other real estate deals, as mentioned above, earning very good returns, and when the opportunity is right, we continue to invest in real estate.

At the time of this writing, the United States is entering another recession, including a housing recession. However, in our position, we are able to hold onto some of the investments and ride through this season. Please do your market research before choosing to invest in real estate to fix and flip or to buy and hold as a landlord. Landlords in many areas are not doing well due to rising taxes and insurance costs.

Private Ventures

Taking some calculated risks is necessary to build a wealth portfolio. We've invested in start-up businesses that were then sold for a profit. I'm also a co-founder of Love Fest, which held the first event in 2025. This involved both sweat equity and a financial investment.

Stock Market Investing

Much of our wealth was built from the stock market, and not from day trading. At this time, we don't day trade. We are both Savers in the Money Mojo types, so it's not in our nature to go back and forth moving money throughout the day.

Recently, we made some major moves to get ahead of a possible recession and placed a large portion of our portfolio into safer areas like high-interest savings accounts and Treasury bills. Bills are different than bonds.

Entrepreneurialism – Coaching, Mentoring and Creative Works

As a coach and mentor in the spiritual, mindset, and manifestation space for more than fifteen years, I have had the opportunity to serve many people, earn income, and still meet my personal preferences for freedom and flexibility.

Additionally, more recently, I've helped women (and a few men) with fitness and nutrition as a certified personal trainer and nutrition coach, after going through my own wellness transformation. I also collaborate with others in an intrapreneurial way, as my priorities are freedom and time, so less personal responsibility for everything, can mean more life and abundance for me.

Being a writer and creative, my projects offer another container for money to flow through and can be activated to increase the flow of abundance. Some of these books connect to my coaching work, and some are purely creative (fiction, poetry).

★★★

Everything on this list can be done while holding a regular or traditional job. People often frown on a corporate or traditional career, but a corporate career served us well, allowing for lifestyle flexibility and my space to be entrepreneurial as a creative and coach.

The other ventures are things anyone can do without considering themselves an entrepreneur. Though a limited liability corporation can come in handy for certain things.

I have an entrepreneurial spirit, and I believe entrepreneurship is a great way to gain financial independence. I've walked in entrepreneurial circles for years, done coaching, courses, and programs, and I have seen that for many, the freedom and independence they seek can cost them their health and relationships. It's a cost that many people only fully realize once they are deep in it.

Entrepreneurship is more than making a product or having a service. It requires having great business sense, marketing skills, people skills, energy, the right money mindset, work ethic, and so much more to become and remain profitable. It works for those who are willing to do the hard work and stick with it long-term and who can manage the risks. For many entrepreneurs, it's both a mindset and a lifestyle.

As an entrepreneur, I approach my work with a lifestyle first approach. I prioritize my freedom and value my flexibility and time. The way I do my work and offer my services has to fit my personality and my vision for a life that is more than just financially rich.

For example, I love wellness and helping people achieve their goals in that area, but building my own business from scratch in this area isn't how I'd like to spend my time. Instead, I find ways to serve that allow me to maintain my values and priorities. That may mean partnering with others, intrapreneurialism, or some other method.

There are those with an entrepreneurial spirit who choose to simply add some additional income on the side using their gifts and talents. For years, as a coach who took a very spiritual approach and as a healer, I did this. While I still incorporate this into my money mojo mentoring programs, I do it in my way.

As a fiction writer, while I might buy a couple of cups of coffee through my stories, I'm not making a living off of them. But, as a writer, I have a hard time not writing, so I write, and since I write, I might as well publish. As I said at a conference I spoke at, it's a serious hobby, perhaps a bit of an addiction, and most of us will feed it.

Come to think of it, I'm feeding it right now. But this time, it's more than a hobby since I know this is a small but mighty book that will change lives. I enjoy writing, but I fully realize that not every side hustle has to become a full-time job. And not every hobby has to be a side hustle. There are some things we do simply because they bring us joy.

If you choose to go the entrepreneurial route, try to get a good sense of what it takes. Talk to entrepreneurs about what it looks like behind the curtains. What you see online is the front of the house and what they want you to see.

There is always more than what you can see from that angle. If your goal is to spend more time with your family and have time for yourself, what is the best option to help you get there if you do need to work while creating your ideal life?

Potential earnings can come from many different sources. If you use the companion *Money Mojo Workbook,* you'll see that you can list not just a regular income but irregular income and earnings as well. Think outside of the traditional sources of income for how you may be able to generate more money.

If you're interested in manifestation, I have a short yet powerful book and a challenge, *Manifest Money in a Month,* with my proven manifestation technique, which I've used to create my own life of abundance and freedom.

Chapter Six

Conscious Savings and Spending Plans

To start creating more financial security by having more money, you have to be mentally aligned with it and have a way to hold it in your life. You also have to be mindful of what is already coming in and going out.

Do you know your family's current monthly income? What are your monthly expenses? How much are you paying on debt, such as student loans, car loans, mortgages, credit cards, and other interest-charging accounts? How much are you making from your money from your savings or interest-bearing (pays you interest) accounts?

Knowing what's really going on with your finances can be scary, especially if paycheck to paycheck is your reality. In addition to what's in this chapter, I have some suggested activities that include this near the end of the book.

I am not a fan of budgets, and most of us groan at the mention of the word. However, I am all for a good conscious savings and spending plan. So, while I do teach about budgets, I take a different angle.

A conscious savings and spending plan considers your values and allows you to put priority on certain expenses over others, consider sources of income that are available and could become available, pay off debt, and build savings into the plan without giving up every bit of joy forever.

According to the National Financial Educators Council, a budget is "a finance plan that allocates future personal income toward expenses, savings, and debt repayment." A conscious savings and spending plan is like a budget, but with a more mindful approach. Your plan includes three primary components: income, expenses, and savings.

- **Income:** This is any cash coming in and includes your paycheck, side hustles, interest from savings, stock dividends, you name it.

- **Expenses:** This is all the money going *out.* This includes rent or mortgage, groceries, car payments, insurance, clothes, your TV/internet, utilities (power, gas, water), that ever-present cellphone bill, and debt payments.

- **Savings:** This is what's left after you pay your

> bills. If you're spending more than you earn, you're racking up debt. If you're putting away more than you spend, then congratulations, you're building up your savings! This can be straight-up cash, but also things like stocks, bonds, or even precious metals. Just please, don't keep the cash in the mattress.

At its core, a budget is just a quick way to compare how much money you're earning versus how much you're spending or saving. In the *Money Mojo Workbook,* you can fill in your expenses to see where your money is going. You'll also fill in your debt as well as a savings plan. After completing these exercises, you'll create a simple conscious savings and spending plan.

Conscious Strategies for Your Savings and Spending Plan.

A good conscious savings and spending plan is essential to taking control of your financial future. While the traditional "budget" might feel restrictive, several popular strategies can help you create a plan that works for you. Here are a few to consider:

The 50/30/20 Rule

This is a simple and flexible approach that breaks down your after-tax income into three categories:

50% for Needs: This covers your essential living expenses, the things you absolutely can't live without. This includes your housing (rent or mortgage), utilities, groceries, transportation, and debt minimums.

30% for Wants: This is the fun part! These are the non-essential expenses that improve your quality of life. Think dining out, entertainment, hobbies, shopping, and travel. This category allows for flexibility and ensures you can still enjoy life while staying on track.

20% for Savings and Debt Repayment: This is the portion of your income dedicated to building your financial future. This includes contributions to your savings accounts, retirement funds, and paying down any debt beyond the minimum payments, such as credit card balances or student loans.

The 50/30/20 rule is a great starting point, especially for those who feel overwhelmed by detailed budgeting. It provides a simple framework that you can easily adjust as your financial situation changes.

Zero-Based Budgeting

If you prefer a more detailed and deliberate approach, zero-based budgeting might be for you. The core principle of this strategy is that every dollar of your income is assigned a specific job.

The goal is to have your income minus your expenses equal zero. This doesn't mean you have no money left at the end of the month, instead it means you've given every dollar a purpose. For example, if your monthly income is $4,000, you would allocate that entire amount to your various categories: rent/mortgage, groceries, transportation, savings, debt repayment, and even a "fun money" category.

This method requires you to be very intentional with your spending. By planning exactly where your money will go, you decrease the chance to spend your money on impulse purchases or things that don't line up with your conscious plan. It helps prioritize what's most important to you, whether that's paying off debt or saving for a down payment on a house. Zero-based budgeting can be an excellent way to get a clear understanding of your spending habits and take complete control of your finances. It does require more commitment and attention that the 50/30/20 rule but this can be a very good method for anyone who needs to pay close attention to their finances.

The Cash Envelope System

This is a very tactile and visual method of budgeting, often used in conjunction with a zero-based budget. After you've paid your fixed expenses (like rent and insurance), you withdraw cash for your variable expenses (like groceries, entertainment, and gas) and place them into separate envelopes. Once an envelope is empty, you're done spending in that category for the month. This method is highly effective for curbing impulse spending, as it provides a tangible limit to how much you can spend in a given category.

These are just a few of the many ways to approach your conscious savings and spending plan. The key is to find the one that resonates with you and helps you achieve your financial goals without feeling overly restricted.

Saving money is one of the primary reasons why we budget. It also helps us stay on top of spending so that there isn't a need to stress on a daily basis, because you've got your income, expenses, and savings planned out. You can spend and save according to what you've put in your budget.

When you've got a solid budget that's been thoughtfully created, it helps you see where you are overspending and where there may be gaps that your current income simply can't cover. It also helps you see where your priorities are. Putting your spending on paper lets you see clearly what is important for you. Money talks and how you spend it tells your story.

As mentioned above, a conscious savings and spending plan is a type of budget, but it incorporates your priorities and values. It encourages you to create a plan that honors you and what's important to you, in the way of meeting your needs, goals, and even desires.

For example, I shared above how I drove my Chrysler Town & Country for years, well past it being paid for. I could have purchased a new car on credit. But one of our values was not to carry unnecessary debt. We waited until we could buy my car with cash before replacing Bessie.

Creating your conscious savings and spending plan isn't just about cutting back, but is more about forward thinking. It's about looking at the big picture, so the choices you make about money reflect your values and what's important to you.

One of your goals when creating your conscious savings and spending plan is to build a plan that allows for a lifestyle you can afford. There are many necessities and desires competing for our limited dollars. You'll need to determine what you can live on and what will be left for savings. That includes all of your savings buckets, which are discussed in the Savings chapter.

Competing priorities and lifestyle goals can pose a challenge in a world that rewards and then punishes instant gratification. What you see on social media is just a snippet of people's lives. I've learned that people are going into large amounts of debt to appear to live a more luxurious lifestyle than they can actually afford.

I learned of one influencer who took out a personal loan of $10,000 to go on a vacation! Unfortunately, many creditors are willing to provide loans to those who qualify. However, accepting these loans can mean paying the debt off for years, when instead you can save for the vacation, you can afford.

Sure, you may put some of the expenses on a credit card, but if it's more than you can expect to pay off when the next bill is due, it's worth pausing and really considering if that expense will help you meet your goals. You can use your conscious savings and spending plan to build up enough savings for those memorable experiences you desire.

It might play out like this. You have a dream of a luxurious vacation overseas, and that money has to come from somewhere. You can either reprioritize your spending or you can increase your income in order to hit the goal of this experience. You may have to make the difficult decision of pushing back this adventure until you can responsibly save the money.

That's just one example. In general, when looking at our conscious savings and spending, we are choosing to be mindful of what is important to us and what might not be as important.

Once you've figured out what parts of your lifestyle are most important for you to focus on, break them down into three categories:

- Things that give you joy, meaning, and purpose. These can be things that make you feel excited. For me, I enjoy theatre and travel. What about you?

- Experiences you want to have later, but they can definitely wait for now. The luxury vacation might fall in this category.

- Fun gadgets or experiences that would be cool to have, but aren't absolutely essential. You probably don't need a new phone every single year.

Dealing with Plan Busters

It happens every month. An unexpectedly high energy bill, or you spent more on gas than you'd planned for. Perhaps you forgot to build in money for your sister's birthday gift and the cake you said you'd handle. Suddenly, your mindful plan has gone bust.

My suggestion is to try to get as close as possible to what you expect to spend, and then leave some flex money. How much you put in this area will vary person to person, but it's the amount that is left when you've accounted for your normal bills and expenses and your planned savings. That money is for things that bust your plan.

At the end of the month, what's left over goes into your savings. Maybe you were hoping I was going to say you can just spend it, but the goal is financial stability and security, and ultimately more freedom. That takes discipline.

Even as I write this, I'm thinking about the person who just had the thought, "Well, that unplanned meal out I had with the bottle of wine counts." And I'll challenge you that this type of "unplanned" or spurious expense is the kind you can absolutely say no to. And if, for some reason, a hard pass isn't possible, how can you limit the extent of your budget bust?

You will need to make some difficult choices at times when you haven't built this into your conscious savings and spending plan. On the other hand, if dining out and socializing like this is a priority, make sure your conscious savings and spending plan reflect that while still keeping it affordable to your income and other commitments.

Your Lifestyle Values and Vision

After you've got your lifestyle preferences all mapped out, you can look at your conscious savings and spending plan with fresh eyes. You can always cut back in areas that are less important to you so that you can apply more money to those areas that you value more. There is an exercise in the companion workbook that helps you think through your values and your vision.

Just make sure your list genuinely reflects your priorities. There's no shame in cutting back on something less important to you to make sure your spending, savings, and income balance to meet your needs and goals.

And for those financial goals that take a while, like months or even years, you can always come back to them and adjust as needed. Six months after you first decided you wanted that new computer, is it still a top priority? It's your right and your responsibility to review your goals to see if they still line up with your vision, values, and priorities. Your goals should change if your priorities and values shift.

***

I have a client who loves to eat out and try new restaurants. It gives her a lot of pleasure, and to hear her talk about it, you know it does. However, she isn't going to spend a lot on things like hair and makeup.

When looking at her conscious savings and spending plan you can see her values and priorities. Sure, she had to choose two weekends a month to go out instead of every weekend so she could build up her emergency fund, but she didn't have to cut it out altogether.

In a small private workshop on conscious savings and spending, a few of the participants asked about giving things up entirely. For example, one man was worried he would not be able to buy his new sneakers anymore if he did the exercise. I think he would've walked out of the room if I told him he couldn't.

I asked him what else was on his priority list. These are the things that are non-negotiable or nearly non-negotiable. He had season tickets to the Atlanta Hawks as a non-negotiable, and those sneakers. On his goals list, he wanted to save an extra three hundred dollars per month for retirement.

This is the thing about making a Conscious Savings and Spending Plan (CSSP). It's your plan. I couldn't tell him what to do; I could only guide him to write down what was important, look at his numbers, and set his own priorities.

In the end, he decided that instead of a new pair of sneakers every month, he would buy a new pair every other month and consider reselling some of the older pairs as a source of extra income to help pay for the new pairs.

He didn't even touch the season tickets and was still able to get his sneakers, even if he had to delay some of the gratification. After the workshop, he told me that he was going to look at a few other things, like his sneakers, that he could do something similar for.

When you have a goal to save or have more financial security, your conscious savings and spending plan becomes your blueprint for not only getting basic living expenses under control, but also for beating the debt cycle.

Constantly overspending when you have access to credit cards or other personal credit creates a pattern of living beyond your means, a consumption culture, and not constantly kicking the responsibility of your financial wellness down the road. When you can get out of the cycle using a smart plan, you can begin to reduce your current debt obligations, which we'll discuss next.

Chapter Seven

Credit and Debt Management

Credit and debt are closely related, almost like sisters. American consumers carried over 18 trillion dollars worth of debt at the start of 2025, according to the Federal Reserve Bank of New York.

At the same time, student loan balances and delinquencies are rising, and would-be home buyers are finding it harder to qualify for a mortgage.

Credit and debt are the two sides of one coin, and when we use them responsibly, they can add value to our lives. On the other hand, accessing and mismanaging credit can take away from our lives, literally taking money out of your pockets. This is money you could be using to pay debt off more quickly, save for an emergency fund, or invest.

Before we get into managing debt, let's talk about credit because it's the precursor to debt. Think of credit like your financial reputation. It's essentially a lender's way of knowing if you're good for the money you borrow.

When you use credit, you're getting something now with the promise that you'll pay it back later, usually with interest, for the privilege. That interest can be a little or a lot, depending on your reputation or your credit profile. The better your reputation, the less risky you are and the less you'll pay for the privilege of using a lender's money.

Your credit history makes up this "reputation". This history is reported on your credit report. Only three companies in the United States of America report credit history and can provide your credit report. They are Experian, TransUnion, and Equifax. They report based on what lenders or creditors report to them.

Your credit report will have the history of any loans and credit cards you have now and all the way through the past seven to ten years. How long a loan or credit card stays on your report can depend on the type of debt and its status. Your credit history also includes any liens, bankruptcies, or other judgments against you.

The lenders report to the bureaus all of the history and whether payments are late, how late they are, and whether they are in collections or another status. This information is monitored on a monthly basis and will show the status of payment by month. See the resources for how the reports are coded.

Your credit score is a three-digit number that sums it all up, and it's critical to financial wellness because of its impact on other things. But before we get into the impact of your score, here's what goes into it and why.

Payment History

This is probably the biggest piece of the pie. Do you pay your bills on time? Every single time? Consistently missing payments or paying late will tank your score faster than you can say "oops." Paying on time? That's gold. When you prioritize making on-time payments, even if it is the minimum it will help your credit score improve. However, these other factors are also important and they are looked at together.

Amounts Owed (Credit Utilization)

This looks at how much credit you're using compared to how much you have available. If you have a credit card with a $10,000 limit and you've got a $9,000 balance, that's high utilization, and it tells lenders you might be stretched thin. Keeping this percentage low (ideally under 30%) looks much better.

Length of Credit History

The longer you've had credit accounts open and in good standing, the better. It shows stability. Naturally, you will build a credit history over time, so starting young with being responsible means you'll have a stronger credit score sooner. If you've been using buy now pay later services, once these get factored in starting in the Fall of 2025, you may see a bump if you have been paying on time.

New Credit

Opening a bunch of new accounts all at once can look risky to lenders, especially if you suddenly apply for a bunch of different types of credit (like a car loan, a credit card, and a personal loan). A few inquiries here and there are fine, but too many too fast can ding your score.

Types of Credit

Having a mix of different types of credit, like a credit card (revolving credit, where the amount you owe changes) and an installment loan (like a car loan, with fixed payments over time), can actually be good. It shows you can handle different financial responsibilities. But having too many lines of credit, especially if they're all maxed out, is a red flag.

There are two companies that take all of this information to calculate your credit score. You've likely heard of the first, by the name of FICO. The official name is the Fair Isaac Corporation. The second is VantageScore Solutions, LLC. Fair Isaac Corporation is a separate business from the credit reporting bureaus, whereas VantageScore Solutions is a joint venture between the credit reporting bureaus.

The scores they calculate are then used by the three reporting agencies. However, each agency has slightly different weights and therefore slightly different credit scores.

Here's how the two companies, VantageScore Solutions and FICO, weigh your credit history to calculate your score.

VantageScore

- Payment History: 40%
- Length of Credit History and Types of Credit: 21%
- Credit Utilization: 20%
- Current Outstanding Amounts: 11%
- New Credit: 5%
- Accessible Credit Amount: 3%

VantageScore looks at credit utilization, in particular, and weighs it heavily. This measures how much credit you have access to and are using. For example, if you have access to a $5,000 credit card and are using $4,500 of it, you have a high utilization, especially if you aren't paying it off completely each month.

On the other hand, the accessible credit amount is how much credit you have taken out, even if you aren't actively using it. In this case, you may have applied and been approved for three credit cards and a store credit card.

Although you are only using the store credit card, you have access to the others, meaning that at any time, you may choose to use them and increase your level of debt. This is seen as risky for a lender.

While VantageScore considers the utilization and accessible credit amounts, FICO is making a key change to how it calculates it's scores. The scoring still looks at these key areas, however, a major change is coming this fall, driven by the popularity of Buy Now, Pay Later financing (BNPL).

These changes were made under pressure and request by large lenders who felt the current score didn't reflect the reality of credit applicants because it ignored a large area of consumer debt. For a year FICO underwent research and planning to create a score that takes these debts into account.

Below is the basis for calculating your FICO score. However, they will be including BNPL information into their calculations beginning Fall 2025. Initially, lenders will be able to see the original score and the new score side-by-side. This gives lenders a way to judge the impact of BNPL on an individual's credit score.

<u>FICO</u>

- Payment History: 35%
- Current Outstanding Amounts: 30%
- Length of Credit History: 15%
- New Credit: 10%
- Types of Credit: 10%

At the time of this writing, it's not settled yet, but it is possible that lenders will be able to decide whether to use the enhanced score which includes BNPL or the original score. Whichever they choose, both scores will be available so if you use these services treat them like any other source of credit.

Understand Your Credit Score

Your credit score directly impacts your "buying power." It's like a secret handshake that lets you access better deals. Lenders use these scores to decide if they'll lend you money and, just as importantly, *at what interest rate.* This is why the changes to FICO matter.

If you have been a user of BNPL financing and have made on-time payments, this new scoring could actually help you. Many times, marginalized groups are more often to use BNPL and they don't have access to traditional lines of credit.

With this change, you may be able to begin building a credit score based on your use of and payment history with this shorter-term financing.

The opposite is also true. If you use BNPL financing but don't make payments on time and wind up being part of the thirty percent of accounts past due, this can severely damage your credit score.

Estimates are that it can knock as much as 180 points off your score. Those points are essentially dollars you'll have to pay at a higher level to get the same amount of credit dollars as someone with a higher score.

The lower your score, the fewer options you have getting credit at all, even at higher interest rates. There is a point when lenders simply consider a potential borrower too risky.

Credit scores range from a low of 300 to a high of 850. The higher the score, the better interest rates you can get on loans and other forms of credit.

Here's a general idea of the FICO score ranges and what they mean for you:

- **800–850: Exceptional.** You're a (financially responsible) rockstar! You'll get the absolute best rates on everything from mortgages to car loans and credit cards.

- **740–799: Very Good.** Still excellent. You'll qualify for very competitive rates.

- **670–739: Good.** You're doing well. Most lenders see you as an acceptable borrower, though rates might be slightly higher than for "very good" scores.

- **580–669: Fair.** You're in a trickier spot. Lenders might see you as a higher risk, which means higher interest rates and potentially fewer loan options.

- **300–579: Poor.** This means big trouble. It will be very hard to get approved for loans or credit cards, and if you do, the interest rates will be sky-high.

Want to improve your score? There's no magic bullet, no matter what those "Fix Your Credit" signs on the road say. At least none that are legal and won't possibly land you behind bars. Instead, do it the right way, with intentional and consistent effort. Here are a few tips for taking care of your credit.

1. Pay everything on time, every time. Set up auto-pay if you need to!

2. Keep your credit utilization low. Pay down those credit card balances.

3. Don't open too many new accounts at once. Be strategic.

4. Check your credit report regularly for errors. You can get a free report annually from AnnualCredit Report.com.

A good credit score is a tool that helps you get ahead in life because of it's impact on total payment amounts. It can mean the difference of hundreds of dollars each month in interest payments compared to someone with better credit.

That will not only add up to serious losses to your bottom line. It also means that money being paid in interest to a lender isn't being used for something better that serves your goals, like paying down debt, saving it or investing it.

Managing Low Credit Scores

What if your credit score isn't on the higher end? First, don't panic and go running to the first person selling a quick fix to your credit. You can fix it. It comes down to two main things: dealing with the past (those negative marks) and being a good credit citizen going forward. What you have to do is build a better credit profile, month by month.

The best ways to boost your score are pretty straightforward:

- Pay on time, every single time. Being consistent with your on-time payments is huge. Both FICO and VantageScore give the most weight to payment history.

- Keep your credit card balances low. Just because you have it, doesn't mean you should use it all. Remember that "credit utilization" we talked about? Aim to keep those balances under thirty percent of your limit.

- Only open the credit lines you actually need. This is about your access to credit. The more access you have, even if you aren't using it right now, the riskier you appear. Don't go applying for every store

> card just because you get a discount. I'm speaking to my younger self right now.

You can also challenge stuff that looks wrong on your credit report. If you see an error, dispute it! It's your right. And if you've really messed up in the past and defaulted on a loan, you might be able to offer a lower payment (an "offer in compromise").

Just know that even if they accept, the original damage is still there, and it'll take time and good habits for it to disappear from your record. I've had to do this in the past to help get from under the weight of a large debt. While it remained on my report, I could pay it off so the damage didn't keep getting worse.

When to Get Help and How to Spot a Scam

Now, while you can repair your credit yourself, you might want some support or professional help. There are companies out there that specialize in credit repair or financial counseling. They can help dispute errors, guide you through debt, or even negotiate with creditors for you.

You may be familiar with debt consolidation or settlement firms. These will be legitimate companies, so check that they are registered with your state to do business and that they have a reputable presence and reviews you can view.

Just remember, these are businesses, and they're going to charge you. They'll probably focus on how much they can save you, but you need to weigh that against their fees. If the savings are greater than their cost, and having an expert in your corner brings you peace of mind, then go for it. But stay vigilant!

There are scams out there. Watch out for anyone who:

- Asks for a huge upfront payment before doing any work. They can take the payment without doing any work, and there will be little you can do about it.

- Wants you to pay in unprofessional ways, like cash, money orders, or gift cards. This suggests that they don't want to leave a money trail.

- Tells you to lie on credit applications. Not only is this fraud, but it can get you in trouble if the lender finds out. It's not worth it. They can file civil and criminal charges, and depending on the offense, you could pay fines or even face jail time.

- Suggests you get a "new" Social Security number. Please don't do this. Lying on your credit application might land you in jail when you are found out.

If anything feels off, trust your gut and walk away. Protecting your financial future means being smart about who you choose to work with.

Getting a grip on your credit is a critical step towards financial health. When the tool of credit becomes a debt-burden it can mess with your mental health and sense of self-worth, weighing you down like a huge stone on your back rather than what it was meant to be, a stepping stone to a better life.

Debt is Personal

This makes me think of my friend, whom I'll call Shay. She was (and is) a whirlwind of energy, always planning adventures and dreaming big. But underneath that vibrant exterior, debt was gnawing at her.

Credit card bills pile up, student loans for a degree she never completed loom, and the dream of buying a home again after losing hers in the 2008 crash still feels light years away. Especially now with the soaring housing costs. She'll say, "It's like I'm running on a treadmill, working hard but going nowhere." And she is. Sound familiar?

The truth is, debt isn't just numbers on a screen or a bank balance that regularly dips into negative because money is snatched out before even think about saving it. It's emotional and very personal. It impacts our relationships, our sleep, and our overall well-being. It can cause stress that wrecks our health. But here's the good news: you're not stuck, just like Shay isn't.

There's a way out, and it starts with smart money management and a solid plan. She's got a plan now to get back on top of her finances, and so can you. There's nothing fun-sounding about smart money management and solid plans, but you'll feel like life is more fun if you aren't zombified by sleepless nights.

Debt should be manageable before you start to save. Though saving money is the key to financial freedom and security, debt is the thief of your future. The United States of America as a country and the people of the United States both have a debt problem. Debt is outpacing our ability to pay it, and creating a debt cycle that makes it hard to exit.

If there is one thing that keeps people in servitude and unable to pursue their career dreams, it's debt obligation. There are what might be considered healthy debts, like a mortgage. But debts today are increasingly unsecured or simply consumer debts. Car loans, student debt, and consumer credit threaten people's livelihoods and financial security.

Yet, we don't have to stay in this trap if we make some critical decisions before getting into debt and are willing to make difficult choices when living with debt. Either way, you'll have to choose what your hard will be. Hard now or harder later? Instant gratification, rising prices, stagnant wages, and a culture that makes it difficult to say no when keeping up with the Joneses is no longer just your neighbor, don't help.

First, let's get real about your finances. If you're sitting under debt, you have to get serious. Do whatever you have to so you can track every penny. Do it every single day. Yes, not at the end of the week or month. Use apps, spreadsheets, or even a good old-fashioned notebook. Knowing where your money goes is the first step to controlling it.

That means you are forced to get tough with yourself and tough on your debt. And you can. In my *Money Mojo Workbook* is a section for paying down your debt.

Paying Down Debt

There are two main ways to pay down debt. Both are described below. Pick a method that works with your personality and needs. If you like immediate wins, the Snowball method may be a good fit. If you have high interest rates, you may benefit from the Avalanche method.

The Avalanche Method: This strategy focuses on paying off debts with the highest interest rates first. By tackling the most expensive debts, you save money on interest in the long run. Research shows that paying high-interest debts first saves a considerable amount of money over time.

The Snowball Method: This method prioritizes paying off the smallest debts first, regardless of interest rates. The psychological boost of seeing those small balances disappear can provide powerful motivation. A study published in the Journal of Consumer Research indicated that small wins can significantly increase motivation in long-term term difficult tasks, such as debt repayment.

Sarah, a client who I worked with to get out of debt, chose the snowball method. She needed that quick win to stay motivated. Seeing those smaller debts disappear gave her the momentum to tackle the bigger ones. It also knocked things off her credit report, which was a psychological boost.

Several years ago, I met a young woman seriously buried under debt. I'll call her LJ for her privacy.

Shortly after the pandemic, I began working with LJ. Initially, she came to me because she wanted to move out of her studio and into a one-bedroom apartment in a better neighborhood. There were a lot of newer apartments in west Midtown.

After touring a few, she paid the high application fee for one she fell in love with. Her application wasn't approved because her debt-to-income ratio was too high and her credit score was low. The combination meant she would have to wait.

LJ was initially going to give up. At twenty-eight, she wasn't sure what to do. She had a decent job, but between student loans and several fun years after college, she'd accumulated what felt like a mountain of debt. She figured she would be stuck in what she called a "crap studio" for another five years.

When we first talked, I asked her about her goals, and she mentioned moving to a new apartment and what she'd come up against when she applied. Then LJ got quiet. She admitted that she didn't want to get stuck.

I asked her what she meant by getting stuck, and she told me about a cousin who had gotten into serious debt and never seemed to move forward in life. This was a cousin she used to admire, but was now stuck in the same life and cycles her cousin had been at the age of twenty-seven. LJ was scared she would get stuck too.

After more conversation, I told her she didn't have to be stuck and that she could get into the apartment she wanted if she was willing to do the work. Again, there was silence.

Then she said, "I don't want to start my thirties like this. What do I need to do?"

Her life began to change that day. It wasn't overnight, and it wasn't always easy. Together, we built a conscious savings and spending plan that prioritized paying down debt, starting with some of her higher-interest credit cards and getting caught up on her student loans. I let her know that if she stayed delinquent, at some point, the government would start counting that against her credit.

Paying off the credit cards would do three things for LJ. First, it would reduce her overall debt-to-income ratio, giving her more breathing room so she wasn't as overleveraged. Second, it would allow her to pay off the debt responsibly, so it would improve her credit profile and score. And third, it would reduce her monthly debt payments, which she could then use towards saving for her new apartment.

It took LJ about one and a half years to do it, but her goal of being in a nicer one-bedroom apartment by the time she was thirty drove her. Along the way, she met someone special. Her vision for her life got even bigger.

No, it wasn't easy, and it took sacrifice, but she wouldn't change a thing. She made a plan, did the work, and met her goals.

If you want to get out of debt, you'll have to make changes and probably some difficult choices. The first thing you'll need to do is make your plan. Again, the free workbook I have can help you make a plan that works for you. In general, you'll need to plan your path to get out of debt, which includes:

- **Setting Realistic Goals:** Don't try to eliminate all your debt overnight. Break it down into manageable chunks.

- **Creating a Debt Payoff Schedule:** Write down your debts, their balances, and interest rates. Choose your method (avalanche or snowball) and stick to it. Consistency is key for both getting rid of debt and improving your credit profile.

- **Finding Extra Income:** Consider a side hustle or selling unused items. Every extra dollar counts. As someone with likely ADHD, I have so many ideas that I could never do. What ideas do you have that excite you?

- **Celebrating Small Victories:** Acknowledge your progress. It's a marathon, not a sprint. Celebrate in ways that make sense and don't set you back.

Once you pay down debt to a manageable level, resist the urge to add to your debt with credit cards, revolving loans, or other debt. When you consistently pay your debt on time and start paying it off, you'll have the added benefit of improving your credit, which is almost like getting a bonus, when it comes to money.

Chapter Eight

Savings

If your car needed four new tires, what would that mean for your finances? How would it impact your livelihood? Could you pay it and pay your regular bills without going into debt? Having savings might seem obvious, but statistics show that most people don't do this consistently.

Most Americans can't manage a $400 emergency and live paycheck to paycheck. This kind of lifestyle puts you more at risk of adding to your debt if any emergency or unexpected expense comes up.

When debt is under control, it's time to start saving your money for your future. Without saving and investing, the chances of you achieving the freedom and financial security you want are low. There are three main buckets of savings that should be funded.

- Emergency Savings
- Long-term Savings

- Short-term Savings

All three play important roles in your quality of life. If you have no savings at all, start with your emergency fund since it can be a lifeboat in the event of job loss, medical needs, or even failed brakes. Your *emergency fund* should be used only for emergencies that impact your ability to live, work, or meet your essential needs.

Your *long-term savings* will eventually be used for your investments. What you choose to invest in is up to you, but having money to invest is important.

While saving, try to earn some interest, even if it's minimal, until you can earn more. Long-term savings in a high-yield savings account you don't take out of will help this fund grow faster.

Your *short-term savings* are more flexible. You can use this money for holiday spending, vacations, celebrations, reunions, birthday gifts, electronic purchases, and other larger purchases that you can save for. When you do this, not only do you get the good feeling that you paid for it, but you also paid without adding to your debt or getting a loan.

Each savings type should have its own account, and if possible, you should set these accounts up to be paid when you are paid or to have a portion of your earnings automatically deposited into them. If you aren't using a credit union or a bank, start researching ones that offer fair or no fees and can accept automatic payments and transfers to make this easy.

If you are working, start with your employer's savings or retirement plan, at a minimum. If you can't get into an employer's plan, set aside your own money in a separate savings account.

It has been generally recommended that you have at least six months of savings in an emergency fund in case of job loss. However, that number isn't going to be enough for everyone. Depending on your career field, you may need more time to allow for a slower job market or time to retrain so you can have more opportunities.

For your long-term savings, you should save enough to so that you get a point where you can take it out of a regular savings account and put into an account that bears higher interest, or take some out to invest in other places like stocks, for a higher return.

Aim to save ten percent of your money each month to begin funding your emergency savings. This may seem high but with the rising costs, having this cushion can help make the difference in keeping your home or vehicle. Once you have your emergency savings in place, y

You can begin funding your long-term and short-term savings with that ten percent. If you can do more than ten percent, do it. If ten percent is more than you can manage, try another amount or a flat dollar amount until you can manage more.

Simple Ways to Start Saving Now

According to a 2023 Lending Club report, sixty-two percent of Americans live paycheck to paycheck, making big savings feel impossible. We're not aiming for a financial miracle here, though I am all about those miracles from our money mojo. Right now, I'm talking about starting with a little nudge in the right direction, to get you going. I'm talking just one percent. I know literally one penny for every dollar. You got this.

To get started, set up an automatic transfer to a separate account. You won't even miss it. If you get paid in cash, such as tips or through services, pay your future self before spending it on anything that isn't essential, starting with that one percent. This works because it gets momentum going in the right direction. Once you see it working, you'll feel much more motivated.

At the time of this writing, the average American household carries a staggering $170,000 in debt. (Federal Reserve Data). This amount of debt hanging over the average family means less money for saving.

It means rainy day funds don't exist, and long-term savings that can roll into retirement savings aren't enough to live off of. This is especially true when Social Security is expected to no longer be sustainable by 2037, with new estimates showing it may run out as early as 2033.

This is why starting now, wherever you are, is better than ignoring this or putting it off for another month or year.

Once you've got the one percent savings going, you can continue. If you can start higher than one percent based on your current spending plan and income, start higher. Don't do the minimum just because you can.

Even if you can afford to save more, this isn't about saving every extra penny you've got. You can if you want, but drastic changes usually don't stick. Building this habit up slowly and steadily will make the behavior last.

We're not trying to be superheroes here. Let's just nudge things in the right direction, bit by bit. You'll want to bump up your savings by another one percent every month or few months. At a minimum, aim for at least a quarterly increase in your savings rate. When you do this consistently, you'll be surprised how fast it adds up.

When you take the approach of starting small, at one percent at a time, it can feel less overwhelming than trying to save a ton all at once or even the recommended ten percent.

But let me say, don't save just one percent if you have it in your conscious savings and spending plan to save more.

If you can save ten percent, which is the ideal amount, or even five percent, aim for the higher rate. Don't take the easy route just because you can.

If you're feeling like there isn't any money to save, even one percent, it's time to do some detective work. You're falling into the ditch of 'where's my money going?' because you either aren't making enough to cover expenses, or you are simply spending more than you think you are.

Let's be real, sometimes we have no clue where our money disappears. It can be scary to take an honest look, but get out your notebook and detective lens. It's time to get into the details. This tip of playing detective means finding those money leaks, so we can plug them up. You'd do the same if you found a leak in your house or under your car's hood, right?

Someone who wants good money mojo and money skills will do the same with their money. Getting a handle on your spending means you have to pay attention to it. If you're not used to tracing your spending and income, try writing down everything you spend in a week. Yes, it includes the vending machine snack at two o'clock or the dollar you gave to someone as a gift.

Once you've got a solid week of information, you can dig into your data. See where you can cut back. That daily six- or seven-dollar latte? Maybe skip it a few times.

Unfortunately, you can't fix what you don't know. Once you see the leaks, you have the problem and can now solve and fix them.

Will you want to splurge on a meal out, to see your favorite team play the team you will loathe for life, or on something new for your wardrobe? You will. I want you to remember at those times that you have a reason for putting this money away.

Your future self will thank you for being disciplined and for caring enough about them to do what it takes now. I understand how hard it is, but temptation is the thief of your dreams and your savings goals. You set your priorities and values, and those special activities, like the ones above, you can do when they are a part of your short-term savings.

When you take a few simple steps to make saving money easy, so you don't have to think about it, you set yourself up for success. The easiest thing to do is to automate transfers to your savings. You can do this through your payroll deposits by having a set amount of money, like one percent or even five percent, automatically deposited into a savings account you've created.

If this isn't an option, you can schedule an automatic transfer to savings on the same day that your money is deposited or make a cash deposit to your savings account when you are paid. There is no reason not to do this when you've set up your conscious savings and spending plan and have carved out this money to save.

The best advice is to automate those transfers! Out of sight, out of mind. That way, you won't be tempted to spend it. Automating your savings removes the emotional element. You're less likely to spend what you don't see. It takes the willpower out of it so you can save on autopilot.

That future version of you wants to be able to say thank you to the current version of you for taking great care of them. That will take long-term thinking. Think about your long-term financial goals, like retirement. Even small savings today add up over time. Picture that comfy retirement for yourself and create a clear vision for your future.

Yes, retirement might seem like a lifetime away for some of you, but years pass quickly, and money needs time to grow. A Transamerica study found that the median retirement savings for Americans in their fifties is only $89,000, while other reports show people between forty-five and fifty-four have on average $115,000 saved.

If you really manage your dollars, that money might get you through three years in the United States of America. It means rainy day funds don't exist, and long-term savings that can roll into retirement savings aren't enough to live off of.

It's suggested that a person who is fifty has six times their annual income, at that time, in retirement savings in order to reach ten to twelve times their income by the time they retire.

My strong suggestion is to start now, wherever you are. It is better than delaying it. Max out what you can contribute to your IRA, especially if you have an employer to gives you a match. I was speaking with another financial educator, and he joked to some college students we were speaking with that even if you have to eat ramen noodles, max out those contributions.

While it may seem funny, there's some reason to it. That is essentially free money being given to you. If you take advantage of this when you're young, that additional employer contribution on top of your own has more time to grow. Beyond this, seek out a professional financial advisor who focuses on retirement savings or money management.

Even if you don't have wealth yet, go in with the goal that you will have wealth and that you need your advisor to help you create a plan to get there. You'll have to follow the plan and possibly change some behaviors, but saving and investing are a critical part of building long-term wealth and creating freedom.

Perhaps you aren't ready to seek the guidance of a wealth advisor. Even if you aren't, you can still open up that regular savings account at your credit union or bank and start with a set percentage that goes directly into that account each month.

Please seek guidance before taking this step. Talk to your banker or benefits manager at your company. See the resources at the end of the Investing section for a book I think is a great starting point.

The key thing is that you must treat this as savings and as part of your creation of future financial security. Unless you have a true and legitimate emergency – DON'T TOUCH IT!

Christmas, holidays, vacations, birthdays, family reunions, school field-trips, new clothes, new shoes, gifts, etcetera, are not emergencies for the emergency fund. Those are funded by your short-term savings, like Michael did, so he could get birthday gifts and pay for dessert.

Case Study

Mark and Willa (Not actual names, 38 and 29, Married Professional Couple)

Mark, a 38-year-old software developer and Willa, a 29-year-old software engineer, were referred to me by a mutual acquaintance. They had a familiar story of financial frustration. Mark and Willa felt trapped in a cycle of renting. After two years of marriage, they wanted to start a family and have a home of their own. Rising home costs, including insurance and prices meant the goal post kept moving on them.

They blamed inflation, which was a real problem, as well as stagnant wages, and even his family's past financial struggles for their inability to save a down payment. Mark had tried quick fixes, hoping for a windfall or a secret investment strategy that would magically solve their problems.

Initially, Mark and Willa couldn't see what they could do. All they could see were the problems they were faced with and felt no control over. Mark's money mojo type was Spender but Willa was a Seeker. When we looked at how they both approached money we were able to make a plan that matched them and let them both take ownership of what they could, based on their strengths.

They had done courses and used apps, but it was when they took personal responsibility for their dreams and their actions, things started to change. They made a plan that made sense for their personal situation. It included being very intentional about saving money where they could and even choosing to rent long-term, securing a better lease agreement in a home and neighborhood they had wanted to live in. For them, it made more financial sense because they knew the total cost wouldn't change for the lease period and they weren't responsible for the hidden costs of home ownership, like broken appliances, HVAC repairs, and other expensive home maintenance, changing taxes and changing insurance costs.

They were willing to be realistic and pragmatic about their approach to money and how they did their housing.

At this time, they are putting the money they would've put towards a down payment into their retirement savings and earning interest on it, building their own vision for a rich life.

Chapter Nine

Investing and Accumulation

Once you've managed to get your debt under control and save money, you can look into investing your money to earn higher returns. This is when your money starts working for you, and you can begin building wealth.

This is not an investment book nor is it investment advice as investing isn't a fundamental money management topic. I am not an investment advisor or financial advisor or financial planner.

However, I do encourage you to work with an investment advisor once you have enough to invest. I'll also share a few things we consider when investing.

Many people run straight to the stock market to invest, picking individual stocks and hoping they choose a winner. However, historically, index funds have outperformed individual stocks since they've been tracking them. That means your money will likely make more money if you pick an index fund that performs well and doesn't have high fees.

I prefer fees under one percent and ideally under half of a percent. Because index funds (compared to mutual funds) aren't managed, they have lower fees. Vanguard and Charles Schwab both offer platforms for investing with index funds available.

When we were transitioning to using our savings and investment earnings to live on, we worked with a financial advisor. However, think hard about contracting with someone on a monthly basis rather than only using them when you need them.

We diversify our investments into exchanges that hold physical precious metals, like gold and silver, in addition to index funds that have visibility into international markets, domestic index funds, high-yield savings accounts, and treasury bills. We also have money in private equity investments and do some real estate investing as well. In the event of an emergency, it's good to have cash you can get to fast without having to pull out a home equity line of credit, since that has to be repaid.

One tip I would give any new investor is to not invest in anything if you aren't willing and able to lose the investment without hardship. If you put five hundred or five thousand into a deal and losing it would set you back financially, reconsider it.

Now, this is not necessarily the case for investing for retirement since you're playing the long game. Even then, diversify so that if stocks crash like they did in 2008 and are fluctuating as I write this, all your eggs aren't in one basket.

You can also research funds that track your age range so that they change how much risk your investment has as you get closer to retirement. These are age-indexed or target-date funds.

There has been a trend of people playing the market. This is different from day trading, which we don't do either. But there are now influencers who encourage people to buy stocks that are hot.

The idea is that they've already bought this stock, and if they can get enough people to buy into it, they get to cash out, having made money on the difference between what they bought it at and the price they convinced others to buy.

Day trading is buying and selling stocks quickly as they rise and fall throughout the day. The trader opens and closes orders, or positions, within a single business day. If they are using borrowed money to do this, it is imperative to close out by the end of the day so they don't pay interest.

This can seem exciting, but be risky, and you might find yourself with a high tax bill or even losing your home, if you're trading on margins and can't cover them.

We learned a tough lesson one year. We weren't day trading, but we sold a substantial amount of stock relatively soon after purchasing it. We were hit with a shockingly huge capital gains tax bill! That sale happened too soon after the purchase, classifying it as a short-term capital gain, which is taxed at a much higher rate than long-term gains, which apply to assets held over a year.

After that painful mistake, we were much more careful about understanding the tax implications of selling investments too soon. It's a reminder that continuous learning is vital because what you don't know can cost you. We found out when our accountant notified us at tax time, when we should have consulted with him before we sold.

As mentioned above, a really good book for some fundamentals and tips on investing is, *I Will Teach You to Be Rich* by Ramit Sethi, for how he breaks down this topic of investing. I think it's good to get multiple perspectives on topics when it comes to money and life.

Once you've managed to get your debt under control and started building up your savings, you're at a pivotal point. This is when you can begin exploring how to make your money truly work for you, moving beyond just saving to actually building substantial wealth through investing.

This book isn't meant to be a deep dive into the complex world of investments, as that's a whole field in itself, distinct from the fundamental money management we've discussed. However, I do want to share some core principles to consider, and strongly encourage you to work with a qualified investment advisor once you have a solid foundation of funds ready for growth.

Many people, when they first think about investing, immediately picture diving into the stock market, picking individual companies they hope will be the next big winner. It's an exciting thought, but history tells a different story. When you look at the long game, broad market exposure through something like an index fund has often outperformed the vast majority of individual stock picks.

This means that, over time, your money is likely to grow more steadily and reliably if it's spread across a wide segment of the market, rather than betting on a handful of companies.

The reason index funds often make more sense for most individual investors is their nature: they simply track a specific market index, like the overall market, without active management. This hands-off approach translates directly into lower fees, which is a significant win for you because every dollar saved on fees is another dollar working to grow your wealth.

When considering any investment, I always look for fees well under one percent, ideally under half a percent. Those small percentages can eat into your returns over the years.

When my husband and I were getting to the point where we were considering using our savings and investment earnings to support our lifestyle, we found it helpful to work with a financial advisor. They offered guidance on structuring our portfolio for our specific goals. However, it's worth thinking carefully about how you engage with an advisor.

There's a difference between a firm that charges a monthly or annual percentage of your assets versus one you consult on an as-needed, hourly basis. The latter can often be more cost-effective for specific questions or annual check-ups, especially once you feel more comfortable with your strategy.

A cornerstone of smart investing is diversification. This isn't just a fancy term; it's a practical way to manage risk by not putting all your eggs in one basket. We aim to spread our investments across various categories.

This includes funds that give us exposure to international markets, as well as those focused on our domestic economy. We also hold assets in physical precious metals, such as gold and silver, which can behave differently from stocks during market fluctuations. We utilize life insurance products that provide growth indexed against funds like the S&P 500 but without the risk of loss in down years. We also use long-term savings vehicles like annuities, rather than certificates of deposits (CDs).

Beyond growth-oriented investments, it's also important to have accessible funds for emergencies. This means maintaining high-yield savings accounts or even holding stable assets like treasury bills.

The goal is to have cash you can access quickly without having to borrow against your home equity, which is debt that needs to be repaid and could put your home at risk if things go sideways. Diversification is about balancing potential for growth with protection against downturns in any single area.

One tip I would offer any new investor, which I've learned the hard way, is this: never invest money if you aren't willing and able to lose that investment without it causing genuine financial hardship. If putting five hundred or five thousand dollars into a deal, and not getting it back, would set you back significantly or create stress, reconsider.

This rule is especially critical for shorter-term investments. It's important to understand your risk tolerance since there are people who invest in stocks that almost treat it like gambling. They may win big, but lose just as big, or bigger.

For long-term goals like retirement and long-term care needs, the approach is slightly different because you're playing a long game where markets tend to recover over years and trend up over decades. Even then, diversification remains key. If the stock market crashes, as it did in 2008 and has experienced other dips even as I write this, you don't want all your eggs in one basket. This is one reason we leverage some of the tools we do. It's also why I suggest not just having your money in retirement savings that can lose value when the stock market does.

You also may want to consider how you'll secure your retirement in a way that ensures you don't outlive your money and can hedge against inflation. For us, we use high-yield savings accounts for easy access to money while outpacing inflation as well as insurance products with long-term care benefits to serve this purpose.

You can also research funds designed to adapt to your age range, often called age-indexed or target-date funds. These funds automatically adjust their risk level, typically becoming more conservative as you get closer to retirement, so you don't have to manage those shifts yourself.

In today's interconnected world, there's a strong trend of people getting involved in the market, often influenced by online personalities. Some individuals influence their followers to buy stocks they say are suddenly "hot."

Often, in these cases, the influencer has already bought shares at a lower price, and if they can convince enough people to jump in, the demand drives the price up. They can then sell their shares for a quick profit.

This kind of activity is speculative and can leave those who bought in later holding the bag when the initial buyers "cash out." It's a risky game to play, and it's essential to understand that not everyone has your best interests at heart.

This is different from traditional investing, and it's also distinct from day trading, which is another high-risk activity we avoid. Day trading, buying and selling stocks rapidly throughout the day to profit from small price movements, can seem thrilling, but it carries significant risk and can lead to a surprisingly high tax bill.

There are day traders who successfully earn money and if you want to go this route, ensure you seek a trusted and legitimate mentor with proven results over time. Look beyond a single day's or a week's wins and losses. How have they fared over months, a year, or longer?

Ultimately, investing and finding ways to accumulate more money using money you already have is a journey of continuous learning. While I've shared some considerations here, remember that getting multiple perspectives on money and life topics is always a good idea.

For some solid fundamentals and practical tips on investing, I've found books like "I Will Teach You to Be Rich" by Ramit Sethi to be helpful in how they break down complex topics. The more you educate yourself and seek diverse viewpoints, the more empowered you'll be on your own financial path.

Chapter Ten

Protecting Your Rich Life

As you build the foundation for your rich life, including the skills that will lead to having more money and assets, you'll reach a point where you'll start asking how to protect it. In the last chapter, we talked a bit about investing, and in this chapter, we'll talk a little about ways you can protect what you've worked so hard to build through insurance. I'll also touch a little bit on protecting your lifestyle as you age.

Is Protection Necessary

The answer to this question is, maybe. Everything depends on your situation and your needs and what you're trying to protect.

Mortgage protection is a popular insurance coverage that takes care of an expense like your mortgage if something happens to the person in your home who pays the mortgage. Is it necessary or required? No. And you might be saying that you already have mortgage insurance. You do, but that's to protect the mortgage company or lender, and not you. They'll get some part of their money, but you aren't in the clear. You're paying their mortgage insurance, but who's covering you? Unless you are, no one is.

So in this case, it's not necessary, but the risk of your family losing your home if something happens to the person who pays the mortgage means you may want to have it.

You can use a similar protection for other debts that would require payment if the primary person who pays for them is no longer here.

What about other more commonly known protective tools like life insurance or senior protection, or long-term care? Are these necessary? Technically, no. The law doesn't currently require you to have any of these, but can they be helpful and provide both protection of the life you've built and create generational wealth? Yes to both.

In the Real World

In 2021, my aunt passed away with no insurance, after being ill for a while from a chronic health condition. Her children were forced to delay the burial in order to fundraise for her funeral. I donated money to help her have a deserving service, as did other family members.

Think about this. Is that how any of us want to leave our loved ones? Essentially, begging during a time of grief for help for something we all know is inevitable? Whether she'd been sick or not, she was nearing eighty years old, and at some point, there would be final expenses. It wasn't necessary that she had insurance, but it would've helped ease the transition and even pay some expenses that came from caring for her.

My own mother purchased life insurance when we were kids because, as a single mother, she knew if something happened to her, there was no one else, and she wanted to make sure we were okay. She still has the policy, paid up, and even though we could take care of her final expenses, she has a policy in place so that instead she can give one last gift to her grandchildren.

When I think of senior protection and life insurance, taking care of those end-of-life needs we know are coming is something I think about. There's also protecting your money when you don't know exactly how long you'll live. Life spans are increasing, and women typically live longer than men, meaning there are more years after retirement than there once were.

On top of this, there are fewer jobs that have a lifetime pension, social security benefits aren't guaranteed, and long-term care needs outpace inflation. At the time of this writing, long-term care facilities can cost $7,500 or more per month. You can see what the estimates are for your area at

In my home, we've taken advantage of long-term care in particular. We've combined an income-producing life-insurance policy with an added long-term care benefit so that we protect our money from being eaten away by long-term care services.

There are stories of individuals with a few million dollars before long-term care expenses winding up with just a couple of hundred thousand dollars once all was said and done. That's money gone that can't be passed down as generational wealth. What's the point of creating that rich life if you can't pay it forward?

Are You Ready?

If you're in the United States, there's a seventy percent chance you'll need long-term care at or after age 65. Many people think long-term care just means a nursing home, but it can mean everything from your child coming by to help you take care of yourself and do the shopping a few days a week to being confined to a nursing home. People also often think that Social Security and Medicare take care of this.

According to the official Medicare website (Medicare.gov/coverage/long-term-care) Medicare doesn't, and the Medicare supplements don't, pay for long-term care. They say that you may qualify for it through Medicaid, or you'll have to buy private long-term care insurance.

If you're interested in exploring any of these protection tools, in addition to being a financial educator, I'm a licensed life insurance agent. There are resources at ShermanFA.com where you can learn more about insurance, determine what your needs are, get a free quote, or even schedule time to talk with me.

Many people have insurance through their jobs, and if so, remember that if you leave that position, you need to request to take your insurance with you. This will keep you locked into the coverage you've got, even if the rates increase somewhat.

The reason this is important is that you won't have to go through qualifying for that coverage again. That's the underwriting process. So if you were fifteen years younger and fifty pounds lighter, you get to benefit from that younger and healthier version of yourself.

If you have private insurance, already check your policy against your current life.

- If something happened to you today, would it cover your needs?

- Would it pay off the mortgage and car loans?
- Would your kids still be able to get help going to college?
- Would your family be able to take care of those final expenses, whether it's burial or cremation?
- Would you be able to start building generational wealth by transferring those life insurance benefits to your heirs?

After all, this is one of the few situations in which they can get this kind of money completely tax-free.

As I mentioned, we're doing the combination of life insurance, specifically universal life, and long-term care. My husband happens to be older than me, and I have some long-living family members, so I don't want to run out of money to live or risk losing what we've built due to long-term care. For me, it's personal since I want to set not just my children up for a rich and abundant life, but their great-great-great-great-grandchildren and then some.

Protecting Your Rich Life and Lifestyle

Protecting our rich lives also means protecting the lifestyle we're creating. That should go without saying, but many people work their entire lives and then are forced to live on the limited income of Social Security.

The investments you've had, your work retirement accounts, and long-term savings accounts are all part of what you have available for your later years. However, as we've learned in this century so far, nothing held within the stock market is guaranteed. It can rise and fall based on something happening halfway around the world or a social media post. There are no guarantees on what losses may be.

This may be why those who have maxed out work-based retirement programs or who don't qualify for them based on having too high an income and who want a secure and certain retirement income, turn to other ways to save for retirement. I mentioned annuities previously, and these are self-funded plans that allow you to put money away for future use or put money in and use it immediately, getting a monthly payment that is guaranteed for life.

People who may be self-employed can benefit from annuities because they don't have access to some of the employer-sponsored plans. Anyone who wants to make sure some part of their retirement income is secure and guaranteed may also purchase annuities. They offer a guaranteed and set income that you cannot outlive. At the time of this writing, they defer taxes, which can help since you don't usually collect your annuity until your regular income is lower, so you're in a lower tax bracket. However, annuities are not for everyone or every situation.

What's Right for You?

To that point, be wary of anyone who believes the tool they have in their toolbox is the only tool you need or the one tool for everything. Nothing is going to be the right tool for every need. If it's right for you, that's great, you've got your answer. If not, find the tool that meets your needs.

Another word of caution; if you have an elderly parent who is considering coverage for final expenses or retirement income, participate in the conversation with them when they're meeting with an agent.

It doesn't matter if the conversation is by phone, video conference, or in person; they are all valid ways to meet. Sometimes the conversations cover complicated topics, and maybe the terms have changed since the last time they even considered insurance. Just being there with them to make sure they understand and you understand is important.

At the end of the day, insurance products, including annuities, long-term care, mortgage protection, and regular life insurance, are a very personal choice and one only you can make that choice. If you're reading this and curious what you might need to prepare, check out some of the tools I share on my business website, or reach out to me to get help calculating it. You can find resources as well as contact information on my Sherman Financial Agency website at https://ShemanFA.com/.

Chapter Eleven

Your Rich Life Starts Now

You've made it to the end of this book, and that's a win in itself. But here's the most important truth, this little book is a starting point, not the finish line.

I've laid out the fundamental skills you need to create financial stability and security. It begins with understanding your income and expenses and moves to saving, tackling debt, and thinking about investing. But this is knowledge. The real magic happens in what you *do* with it.

Some folks will read through these pages, nod their heads, and then set the book aside, promising themselves they'll get to the workbook or create their own plan—just as soon as they find some "free time."

Let me tell you something. That free time won't just magically appear. You have to be intentional about carving it out. Life gets busy and distractions pop up.

If you're not intentional about acting on your money goals, they'll remain just good intentions, with nothing to ground them and make them real in your life.

The difference between wishing for financial change and actually achieving it isn't a hard concept. All it requires is making the decision and then applying consistent, intentional action.

Your money skills, your ability to manage, grow, and truly understand your finances, can and will improve, just like your financial situation. This isn't about being perfect from day one. It's about progress.

Progress requires being patient with yourself, understanding that building new habits takes time, learning from every success and failure, and committing to doing what's needed.

As with learning only new skill, you don't become an expert overnight, but consistent practice makes you better, stronger, and more confident.

That's why I want you to make a commitment right now. Choose to do one concrete thing in the next twenty-four hours that will help you build momentum toward making these changes to your money skills and, more importantly, sticking with them.

Think of it as lighting the fuse. Based on your personal situation and most pressing needs, you can pick any item from the suggestions in this book.

If you know you need more income, dive into the income exercise.

If reducing debt is your immediate priority, start there.

If building an emergency fund is what you need most, that's your starting point.

The specific action isn't as important as *taking* an action. Once you complete that first step, move immediately to the next. Keep building on that momentum until you've taken solid, intentional action in every key area of your finances.

This isn't about perfection; it's about progress, one deliberate step at a time, transforming ideas into your new financial reality.

Intentional Money Action Items

Income and Earnings

Write out in detail your current monthly income and any other monthly earnings you receive. Then write down any other income or earnings you get throughout the year.

If you know when you get them (for example, tax returns) write that down too. Add everything up and divide it by twelve to see your average monthly income.

The next thing you'll do will help you see the impact of tax returns on income and the potential for that money to help you reach your financial goals. Repeat the exercise of adding up your income, but leave out any extra earnings you get from tax returns. If you receive bonuses from work, leave those out as well, unless you can reliably depend on them each year.

Now, divide that number by twelve for your average standard monthly income. This is your baseline income. This is the number you should aim to live within or beneath. If you are a commissioned salesperson, this won't apply to you but you should look over the past two to three years of your earnings to establish your average monthly income.

If you've changed organizations or compensation plans in that time, use the most recent plan to average out your earnings. This is a great first step to understanding the money you really have available to use and to meet living expenses and savings goals.

Conscious Savings and Spending

If you already know your income, you can jump in right here with creating a conscious savings and spending plan.

For a free Google worksheet, see the resources at the end of the book or you can search online for 'budget' templates or forms.

You will need to gather your regular expenses and the ones that change from month to month or are billed in some increment other than monthly, such as bi-monthly waste management, quarterly subscriptions, or an annual insurance bill. Use the worksheet I've provided or create your own worksheet and build your plan, based on your priorities. Remember, it's okay to plan for some fun, even if it has to be delayed.

Understand Your Debt

If you have a goal of reducing or eliminating your debt, you can do this one first. However, after doing the plan you may need to revisit your income and even your conscious savings and spending plan in order to act on your debt reduction plan.

If you get the *Money Mojo Workbook*, there is a section on debt management. Because this is such an important area for people, I've also pulled that section on as a free download if you go to bernettesherman.com/debt. You can also revisit the section on Debt Management as a reminder of how to start eliminating your debt.

Start Your Emergency Fund

It doesn't matter how you start, but it does matter that you start. Choose a percentage or an amount to save whenever you get income. Ideally, you can begin paying yourself ten percent, if not, start where you can.

Set up a separate savings account or if you have one that is collecting dust, dust it off now. You can do all of that immediately. Then, if you have a regular paycheck, request that your employer automatically deposit the desired amount from your paycheck into the savings account. If this isn't possible, as soon as the payment clears your bank or you have cash in hand, take out the amount you decided on for savings and put it into the savings account. A jar in the cabinet is not a savings account.

Consider How You'll Protect Your Money

To protect your money and assets, diversification is critical. Like the saying goes, don't keep all your eggs in one basket. If everything is in the stock market or your home's equity and we have a repeat of 2008's Great Financial Crisis, it could upend all of your plans for retirement and passive income. Have a healthy blend for your savings and investments. You may want to consult with an investment advisor who can point you towards a mix that works with your goals.

Don't overlook the value and safety net that insurance provides. If you already have insurance policies or annuities, review their status and whether they still meet your needs and that all contact information and beneficiaries are up to date. You'll also want to review your policy compared to what's on the market now to see if there is a better product that wasn't available when you purchased it. You may wish to update or upgrade your policy if you find you can have better returns, income, or accumulation of your money.

Also look at your planning for not just your own retirement needs, including long-term care, but those who's needs will impact you. This includes family members who might rely on you to care for them as they age. Are they set up with Medicare and the supplements so that they're making the most of their money today and staying as healthy as possible? If they are showing signs of decline are they able to use Medicaid services? If they're healthy but getting older, there are policies that can provide much needed support to family caregivers so you can keep your loved ones at home. For example, my mom has already told me she's moving in with me when she's old.

Protecting your money is the part of the equation that recognizes that building a rich life isn't just about how much you make, but how much you keep. And for a truly rich life, it also includes what you can pass on to future generations.

28 Days of Money Momentum

The best way to be successful is to take immediate action. You can build momentum with your money skills when you start now and do something intentional every single day to reach your goals. Use this time to review the intentional actions from the section above and make a list from one to twenty-eight for each day.

Write down one action you will commit to taking for each day. It could be paying off one of your smaller credit cards or opening a savings account to determine what options you have for increasing your income. You'll probably find that just starting the list with a few ideas will give you even more ideas as your creative juices start flowing.

Set up an accountability system so you stay true to your goals and yourself. It might mean doing this exercise with a friend or partner, setting up reminders in your phone or an app, or being accountable on social media (without providing specific details, of course).

It doesn't matter what you choose, only that you do something so that you can notice your progress and keep that motivation and momentum going. The workbook is a helpful tool to use as you can create goals and work through the pages.

And, I would love to hear from you after you've gotten past the thirty days to see what new money habits you've built and what changes you made to your financial situation.

The Next Step on Your Journey

Once you've applied the practical money skills I share in this book to your life on a consistent basis, you will see extra money in your conscious savings and spending plan. You'll begin to experience having a little cushion, and then savings, and then stability that allows you to move to the next step of your financial journey.

If you are already stable, it's time to get to security. That's where you begin investing your money to earn interest for your long-term financial security. You can also invest in yourself to improve your ability to create even more financial success.

The best thing about getting these skills for your rich life is that when you become wealthy and financially secure, you have time and freedom. You can take care of your body and overall wellness, nurture your relationships, and experience more moments that bring you joy.

You can't compare it with anything else of real value, in my opinion. Truly. Your health, relationships, and happiness all make up your rich life by giving you a higher quality of all your experiences.

We underestimate the importance of time freedom and having the mental capacity, that free space in our mind, to think and dream, and just be. When we finally get to that point of having it, we realize how much we didn't have before.

What if you could have more, in fact have the life you truly want, because more money was flowing into the containers you will create or have already created? What if you could have it with more ease and less stress?

It's possible. As a mentor, I help people do just this. If you're interested in learning the secrets I've used to manifest opportunities and create abundance in my life, be sure to follow me (see About the Author section) for my book Manifest Money in a Month. You can also read the excerpt included after this chapter.

Your Future, Your Power

You have the power to change your financial well-being, and it doesn't take anything more than practical, repeatable money skills. This journey isn't just about numbers on a spreadsheet or keeping up with an app; it's about reclaiming your peace, having flexibility, and opening up possibilities you might not have even imagined.

What's waiting on the other side of taking intentional and inspired action based on your vision for yourself is that richer life. I mean it in the fullest holistic context of that word. Abundance, prosperity, and a life that *feels* rich because you don't lack anything that you value, from love to health to wealth.

When you have that kind of rich life, you feel more secure, freer, and more in control of your own destiny.

You're not stuck. You now have the knowledge, skills, and the power to act. Wherever you are starting from today, it's just the beginning. You aren't a victim of the past, your family, your neighborhood, or the cultural norms you grew up in.

You are an individual with the power to change your life and that begins with knowing and believing you can and then acting in ways that support the rich life you want.

The resources are available to help you move forward, including the *Money Mojo Workbook*, which is designed to guide you through using these practical money skills. For those looking for more support, I encourage you to visit my website, BernetteSherman.com, to explore additional resources and mentoring options.

These are simple skills that can change your life. Will it be easy? For some, it will be. For others, you will feel challenged. Push through the challenge and rise to the occasion that your future self is calling you to. Get these money skills for your rich life.

Friend, that's all I have for you. Your financial future is waiting for you to write its next chapter. It's time for you to start building your rich life.

***

Would you please take one minute to write a review of this book and help others discover the money skills to create their rich life too?

Manifest Money in a Month Book Excerpt

The Proven and Powerful Money Manifestation Technique

Your Money is on the Way

You are here because you want to manifest money faster, and you don't want to read a three-hundred-page book to do it. You may not want to read a book at all, but here we are.

This book is meant to be used with the Manifest Money in a Month Challenge, which you can find through my website, BernetteSherman.com/moneychallenge.

I am telling you upfront, your money is already on the way. It's out there for you. You just need to tell the universe how much, where to deliver it, and make sure it can actually drop off your package.

I'm going to deliver to you what you need in the shortest form possible without eliminating what you need to be successful.

Even if it only helps you ten or twenty percent, that may be enough to elevate your life, help you build your confidence, and get you started on a path to manifesting more money and creating the miracles you seek from life.

Who do you think you are to have it all? A part of a limitless universe, of course, and that universe can give you the money you desire.

What I share can help you get where you want to go faster when you use it as designed.

I can't promise you'll get rich, but you can create, attract, and keep more money in your life.

Manifestation takes consistency and time. While there are ways to bend space and time and collapse how long it takes to manifest (like using the tools I used), you still must remain focused.

You'll see that when we use our mind, spirit, and body, everything can be aligned and you can create miracles for your next level life!

***

This book is meant to be used with the Manifest Money in a Month Challenge. You've decided to change your life and become a true money manifestor, and you chose this challenge to help you do it. That takes courage and courage is no small thing. Congratulations!

How do you use this book to begin manifesting more money and your next-level life? Originally, this program contained five main parts, and the core of those is still relevant. However, I have discovered some simpler ways to manifest, and I am all about having more ease in my life and in how I receive what I desire.

Ideally, you can commit to a minimum of one month to work through this book and use the tools. Do the release statements, receiving statements, and exercises daily. This is very important. However, I suggest that you give yourself a day or two before beginning the tools so you can read through the materials before you use the tools and also have time to complete all of the exercises in Clearing the Way for Money Manifestation.

Completing these exercises will help focus you when reading and when doing the program. Trust me, you'll be better prepared to get the most benefit from what comes next.

You have the choice to do something completely different, but I'd advise that you don't stray too much from the program as designed.

Before you begin the Manifest Money in a Month Challenge, please consider doing the following:

Dedicate a notebook to be called Manifest Money in a Month. When you enroll in the challenge, you'll get a simple tracking sheet and a one-page version of the main meditation tool. However, a notebook or journal allows you to be more expansive in your thoughts and what you are noticing.

You can also get the money activation sequence or money healing and clearing as a separate service by visiting the appointments page on my website at BernetteSherman.co m/appointments.

Your Manifestation Practice

The practice of manifesting and the amazing life that comes with it takes discipline and time. It may not happen next week if you are just starting out today. However, it could.

Like anything else in life, you want to get good at, it will take time and energy. If you are learning a new skill, training in a new professional field, or taking up dance after a twenty-year break, understand that it takes practice, over and over. Sometimes you might do quite well, and sometimes you'll make mistakes. Don't give up! Keep at it.

While this book is for manifesting money in thirty days, being a manifestor is a lifelong trip, and you'll only get better with time and practice. I'm still learning, growing, and working on my practice as well. It doesn't always work like I had planned, and I've been working on my practice for most of my life, even when I wasn't fully aware. I've been doing it knowingly for over fifteen years.

If things aren't going as easily as you'd like, go easy on yourself. You've got a whole life to live outside of learning to manifest, which is just a fancy word for learning to become the master over your mind, your feelings, your actions and what you create.

There is great power in all of those! And because there is so much power, you need time to get used to the power, go to the next level (think of it like going to different grades in school), and become a responsible and more powerful money manifestor.

Vision and Goals

Being intentional about manifesting money in a month means that you must have a goal and work towards it purposefully over this period of time. You may not make a complete transformation in thirty days, but you can keep repeating it, seeking higher results each time.

It is a transformation and moving out of a consciousness or state of mind that sees poverty, lack, and not having enough as normal, rather than knowing that abundance is just as normal, if you choose. Having more money and abundance is within your grasp.

***

Enjoyed the excerpt: Get it now or join the challenge at BernetteSherman.com/moneychallenge

Resources

Financial Coaching (The Money Mojo Mentor):
BernetteSherman.com
Sherman Financial Agency:
ShermanFA.com
Manifest Money in a Month:
BernetteSherman.com/moneychallenge
Talks and Events:
BernetteSherman.com/my-events
Money Mojo Workbook:
BernetteSherman.com/money-skills
Money Mojo Type Quiz:
BernetteSherman.com/quiz
Free Annual Credit Report:
AnnualCreditReport.com

Credit Report Coding

Each cell in the grid contains a color-coded abbreviation representing the payment status for that month. The legend provides the following information:

- **CLS (Green):** Current/Terms of agreement met
- **30 (Yellow):** Account 30 days past due
- **60 (Yellow):** Account 60 days past due
- **90 (Yellow):** Account 90 days past due
- **120 (Orange):** Account 120 days past due
- **150 (Orange):** Account 150 days past due
- **180 (Orange):** Account 180 days past due
- **CRD (Red):** Creditor received deed
- **FS (Red):** Foreclosure proceedings started
- **F (Red):** Foreclosed
- **VS (Red):** Voluntarily surrendered
- **R (Red):** Repossession
- **PBC (Pink):** Paid by creditor
- **IC (Pink):** Insurance claim

- **G (Red):** Claim filed with government
- **D (Red):** Defaulted on contract
- **C (Red):** Collection
- **CO (Red):** Charge off
- **CLS (Gray):** Closed
- **ND (Gray):** No data for this time period

Also by

At BernetteSherman.com/books-by-bernette

Manifest Money in a Month
Money Skills for Your Rich Life
Money Mojo Workbook
Success is in Your Story
Love Me Journal
Protect and Clear with the Divine
Heaven is Now: Enough Excuses
Resist Persist
But First Crawl (Romantic Comedy)
Light of the Dark Moon (Fantasy)
Star Jumpers (Metaphysical Sci-fi)
The Story of Ervin James (Historical Fiction)
Out of the Woods (Fantasy)
Crossed (Paranormal light urban thriller)

About the Author

Bernette Sherman is the Money Mojo Mentor, a holistic financial coach, money mentor, and author with a focus on helping individuals, couples, and families create and keep financial security and freedom. Bernette has healed generational trauma, a poverty mindset, and broken relationships while creating generational wealth and a philanthropic legacy.

She holds an MPA in Policy Analysis and a Bachelor's in Business from Georgia State University, is an NFEC Certified Financial Education Instructor, and licensed life insurance agent.

Most of her professional work has been in the public or nonprofit sectors, as a writer, and coach. Her goal is to help others create their own rich lives and a generational legacy.

Coaching Website: BernetteSherman.com
Agent Website: ShermanFA.com

Books: BernetteSherman.com/books-by-bernette

Instagram @IAmBernette

Facebook @IAmBernetteSherman

YouTube @IAmBernette

Tiktok @IAmBernette

Made in United States
North Haven, CT
04 November 2026

21772060R00092